MASTER CLASS

ROCK LEAD
Performance

Techniques, Scales, and Soloing
Concepts for Guitar

by Nick Nolan and Danny Gill

PLAYBACK+
Speed • Pitch • Balance • Loop

To access audio visit:
www.halleonard.com/mylibrary

Enter Code
7859-8227-4453-0276

ISBN 978-0-7935-9058-2

7777 W. BLUEMOUND RD. P.O. BOX 13819 MILWAUKEE, WI 53213

Visit Hal Leonard Online at
www.halleonard.com

CONTENTS

ABOUT THE AUTHORS

Danny Gill left and Nick Nolan right.

Nick Nolan comes from Port Huron, Michigan where he began his professional playing career at the age of sixteen. He then went to G.I.T. on the Eddie Van Halen Scholarship and graduated with honors. After graduating, Nick became an instructor at G.I.T., teaching and writing curriculum for such subjects as: Rock Lead Guitar, Rock Rhythm Guitar, and the Rhythm Section Workshop, as well as teaching Music Reading, Harmony and Theory, Ear Training, and Modern Rock Performance.

Nick is also an active session player in Los Angeles, playing guitar on such T.V. series as: "Melrose Place," "Star Search" (as house guitarist), and "High Tide." You may have also heard Nick on the cartoons: "Bill and Ted's Excellent Adventure," "Back to the Future" (CBS), "Where's Waldo?" (CBS), "Super Mario Brothers" (NBC), "Captain Planet" (FOX), "Exosquad" (Universal), "What a Mess" (DIC), "Don Coyote" (Hanna-Barbera), and "The Funtastic World of Hanna-Barbera."

Nick's first CD is titled *Up & Down & Back Again* on Standing 8 Records (P.O. Box 5280, North Hollywood, CA 91616). Check out Nick's website: (www.nicknolan.com).

Danny Gill recorded his first CD in 1990 with Hericane Alice (Atlantic Records). Since then, he has gone on to record and tour with Arcade, Medicine Wheel, and will debut his new band Speak No Evil in 1998 on MCA Records. His songs have appeared on numerous network T.V. shows and major motion picture soundtracks. Danny has also released a Star Licks video entitled *Modern Rock Guitar*. He currently teaches at Musicians Institute in Hollywood, CA; his classes include *Rock Rhythm Guitar*, *Rock Lead Guitar*, and *Single String Technique*.

CREDITS

Nick Nolan: guitar, keyboards

Danny Gill: guitar

Ian Mayo: bass

Tim Pedersen: drums

Recorded and mixed by Dallan Beck, Nick, and Danny. Assisted by Steve Sandpearl, Recorded at M.I. studios, Rubberneck studios, and Crash and Burn studios.

Photos by Kathrin Kraft

Danny thanks: my beautiful wife Alexandra and all of my great family.

Nick thanks: my wife Hiko (for everything), and Rob and Mick at Hoshino (for the great Talman).

Editor's notes:

Follow the audio icons (◆) in the book.

A short "introduction" or "tag" may precede or follow the main lick of each figure to give it a better sense of context. However, only the main lick itself appears transcribed in each case.

CHAPTER 1
MODES

FINDING THE KEY CENTER

I n order to use modes effectively, you must know how to find the key center (i.e. the relative major scale). To do this, you must learn the chords of the harmonized major scale. The harmonized major scale is a group of chords made from the notes of the diatonic major scale. Memorize the order in which the chords occur. The order of these chords (which are major, minor, or diminished) are the same in every key.

Fig. 1

I	II	III	IV	V	VI	VII
major	minor	minor	major	major	minor	diminished

Take a look at this song. See if you can figure out what key it's in:

Fig. 2

Here's a hint: the first chord is usually the name of the key. Not always!—just usually. So, let's start there. Take a look at the harmonized C major scale:

Fig. 3

C major	I	II	III	IV	V	VI	VII
	C	Dm	Em	F	G	Am	B°

Notice how every chord fits in the key. This is a I–II–IV–V progression in C major.

Try the next one on your own. To make your life hard, the first chord is not the key center.

Fig. 4

Answer: A major

If you missed it, here's how it works. There are four chords: D, E, F#m, and A. Let's make note of the three major chords (D, E, and A). Try to fit them into the harmonized scale.

Fig. 5

I	II	III	IV	V	VI	VII
major	minor	minor	major	major	minor	diminished

The only way they'll fit is where A is I, D is IV, and E is V. That would leave F# minor as VI and everything works out.

Let's try one more using triads from the major scale:

Fig. 6 Gm   F   C   B♭

Answer: F major

This one was a little more difficult. If you had trouble, follow these steps closely:

1. Take note of the G minor chord. If we look back to Fig. 1, we know that a minor triad can either be a II, a III, or a VI chord.

2. Now ask yourself, "If G minor is II, then does the F major chord work as the I chord?" Answer: You betcha!

3. Now test the other chords. Is C in the key of F? (Yes, it's the V chord.) And what about B♭? (Yup, it's the IV chord.)

As you can see, it becomes very important to memorize the order of the chords in the harmonized major scale. Get this down cold before moving on to seventh chords.

If we add the seventh scale degree to each of the triads, we get the following seventh chords:

Fig. 7

I	II	III	IV	V	VI	VII
major 7	minor 7	minor 7	major 7	dominant 7	minor 7	minor 7♭5

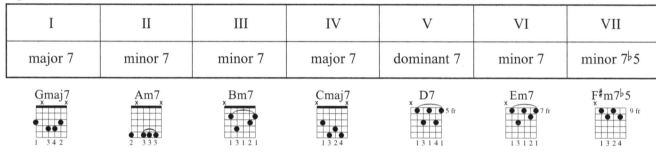

See if you can find the key for this song:

Fig. 8 Gmaj7   Em7   Am7   Cmaj7

Answer: G major

Why G major? Well, let's assume that the first chord is the name of the key. Take a look at the harmonized G major scale in seventh chords:

Fig. 9

	I	II	III	IV	V	VI	VII
G major	Gmaj7	Am7	Bm7	Cmaj7	D7	Em7	F♯m7♭5

All of the chords fit perfectly. This is a I–VI–II–V progression in G major.

Here's one where the first chord is not the key center.

Fig. 10 Dm7   G7   C

Answer: C major

In this progression, the G7 is a dead giveaway. Because the dominant seventh chord can *only* be a V chord, C must be the I chord. Now check the Dm7 chord. Looking back to Fig. 7, we see that the minor seventh chord can be a II, III, or VI chord. In C major, Dm7 is the II chord. This II–V–I progression is used in a lot of songs.

If you can figure out which major key this next tune is in, you're ready to start playing with modes. (Hint: there is *no I chord!*)

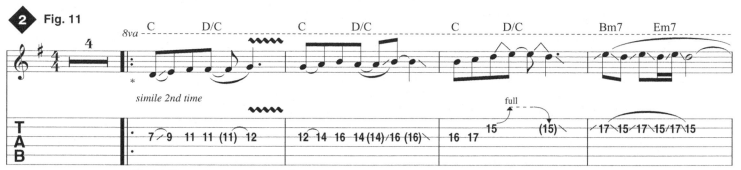

*Doubled by another gtr. one octave lower.

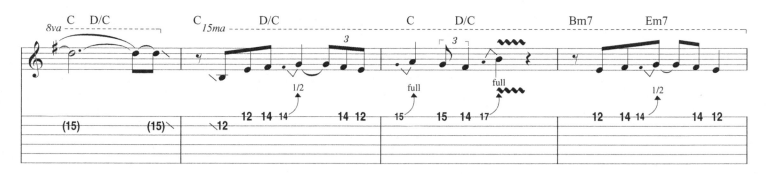

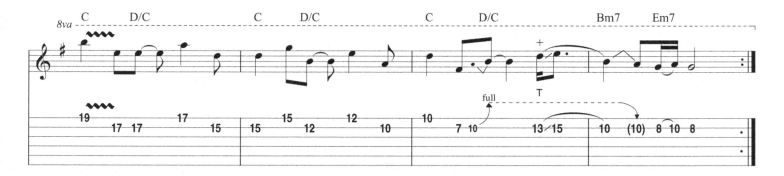

Answer: G major

Why G major? Start with the two major triads. They are one whole step apart. The only place this happens is between the IV and V chord. Now ask yourself: "if C is IV, then what is I?" And the answer is—G major. D/C, Bm7, and Em7 fit in G major? They sure do. Bm7 is the III chord and Em7 is the VI chord. If you still don't believe me, take a long look at Fig. 9 and do your homework!!

Well, I think that's enough talk! Let's jam over the chords from Fig. 11.[1]

---

[1] For a more in-depth look at diatonic scales and their applications, see *Rock Lead Basics*.

CHAPTER 2
MODAL PLAYING

I n our previous books (*Rock Lead Guitar Basics* and *Rock Lead Guitar Techniques)*, we showed you some of the solo situations you're bound to run into. We covered major keys, minor keys, and a lot of pentatonic/blues situations. The next obvious step is modal playing.

Modes are a subject that comes up a lot in our teaching at M.I., and we've found that many students are confused about how to use them in their soloing. What we're going to do here is explain the modes in *three* different ways. We've found this to be the key to understanding and using the modes most effectively.

1. MAJOR SCALES STARTING ON DIFFERENT NOTES

Here's the first thing that everyone learns about modes: if you start and end a major scale on a note other then the tonic, you've created a mode.

G Major:	G–A–B–C–D–E–F♯–G
Starting on a different note:	E–F♯–G–A–B–C–D–E

Above is a perfect example of a mode. We took a G major scale and started/ended on the note "E." These two scales have a different sound and mood. The G scale sounds bright and the E scale sounds darker.

Let's take the above example all the way and start a G major scale on every different scale note.

Starting on G:	G–A–B–C–D–E–F♯–G	(G Ionian)
Starting on A:	A–B–C–D–E–F♯–G–A	(A Dorian)
Starting on B:	B–C–D–E–F♯–G–A–B	(B Phrygian)
Starting on C:	C–D–E–F♯–G–A–B–C	(C Lydian)
Starting on D:	D–E–F♯–G–A–B–C–D	(D Mixolydian)
Starting on E:	E–F♯–G–A–B–C–D–E	(E Aeolian)
Starting on F♯:	F♯–G–A–B–C–D–E–F♯	(F♯ Locrian)

As you can see, there are seven possible modes. What are those names to the right of the scale? Well, the Greeks were the first to name the modes, back in the sixteenth century, and we still use those names today. They go like this:

When starting/ending on the first note:	Ionian (We also call this major)
When starting/ending on the second note:	Dorian
When starting/ending on the third note:	Phrygian
When starting/ending on the fourth note:	Lydian
When starting/ending on the fifth note:	Mixolydian
When starting/ending on the sixth note:	Aeolian (We also call this minor)
When starting/ending on the seventh note:	Locrian

Remembering the order of the mode names is essential to modal playing!

Now that you've seen that modes are really just major scales starting/ending on different notes, it will make learning how to play them much easier. For example, if you want to play *C Lydian*, take a G major scale and start/end on the note C—that's it! (This is assuming that you know your major scales. If not, get back to *Rock Lead Guitar Basics!*)

Translating modes to their relative major is an important step to playing with modes. The process is this:

1) *C Lydian* means "C is the fourth note of the relative major scale" (Lydian is the fourth mode).

2) Count backwards from C to find out what the first mode is.

3) That means C Lydian has the exact same notes as G major: C–D–E–F♯–G–A–B–C.

Let's do one more together: F Mixolydian = _____ major.

1) F Mixolydian means "F is the fifth note."

	1	2	3	4	5	6	7	8

F above 5

2) This time, let's count *up* to 8 since it's closer (8 and 1 are the same note.)

F 5 — whole step — G 6 — whole step — A 7 — half step — B♭ 8

3) The answer is B♭ major.

Translate these modes to their relative major:

1. A Phrygian   = _____ major   6. B Phrygian   = _____ major

2. F Dorian   = _____ major   7. A Lydian   = _____ major

3. B♭ Lydian   = _____ major   8. E♭ Aeolian   = _____ major

4. G Mixolydian = _____ major   9. G Locrian   = _____ major

5. C Aeolian   = _____ major   10. F♯ Mixolydian = _____ major

Answers: *1.) F major*   *2.) E♭ major*   *3.) F major*   *4.) C major*   *5.) E♭ major*   *6.) G major*
          7.) E major   *8.) G♭ major*   *9.) A♭ major*   *10.) B major*

2. COMPARING MODES TO THE PARALLEL MAJOR SCALE

Now that you've seen modes in reference to their relative major, let's find out what the difference is between a mode and its *parallel* major key. A parallel key is one that starts on the same root. For example, C major and C Lydian are parallel keys.

What would you play over this?

4 ▸ Fig. 13 – D Lydian Jam

Fade In

play 6 times

Sure, you could just play D major, but you'd be missing out on a lot of cool, interesting, unique, different, fun, happy, soulful, funky, and groovy stuff. You use spices when you cook, right?—same thing here. Use this stuff to stimulate your palate. Vanilla is good, but not all the time. If it's too spicy, you get heartburn. Get in there and find out what you like. Here we go!

The three modes associated with major sounds are:

1. Ionian (major)

2. Lydian

3. Mixolydian

The Lydian mode and the Mixolydian mode have just one note different from the major scale. Compared to the major, Lydian is a major scale with a ♯4; Mixolydian is a major scale with a ♭7. Emphasizing these alterations will give you that "modal" sound.

D Major	D–E–F♯–G–A–B–C♯–D
D Lydian	D–E–F♯–G♯–A–B–C♯–D
D Mixolydian	D–E–F♯–G–A–B–C–D

Before you start jamming with these scales, let's take a look at five D Lydian and five D Mixolydian scales. I know—they all look like the major scales you've already learned. In fact, they are the major scales you've already learned! But by learning where the roots are, you're more likely to sound like you're playing in that mode.

Fig. 14 – D Lydian Patterns

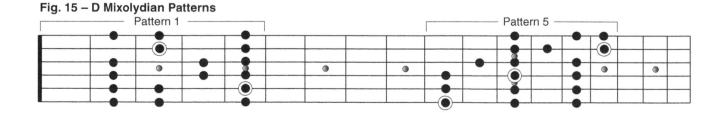

Fig. 15 – D Mixolydian Patterns

Pattern 2

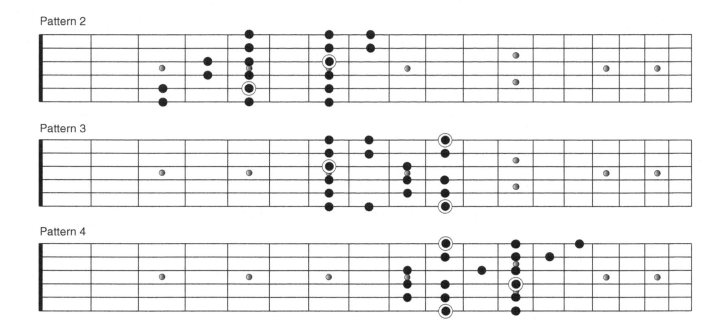

Pattern 3

Pattern 4

And now, finally, let's jam! We'll start with D Lydian.

Mess around over the droning D bass in Fig. 13 (track 4) or cop some of the Lydian ideas in Fig. 16.

5 **Fig. 16 – D Lydian Solo**

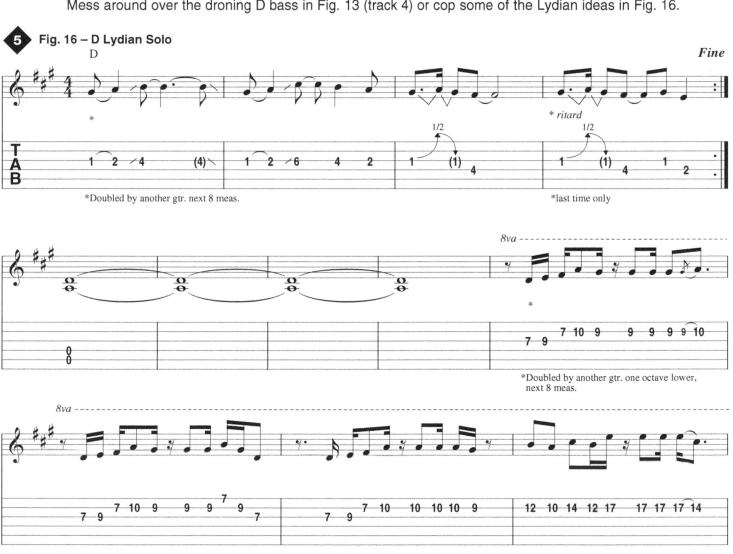

*Doubled by another gtr. next 8 meas.

*last time only

*Doubled by another gtr. one octave lower, next 8 meas.

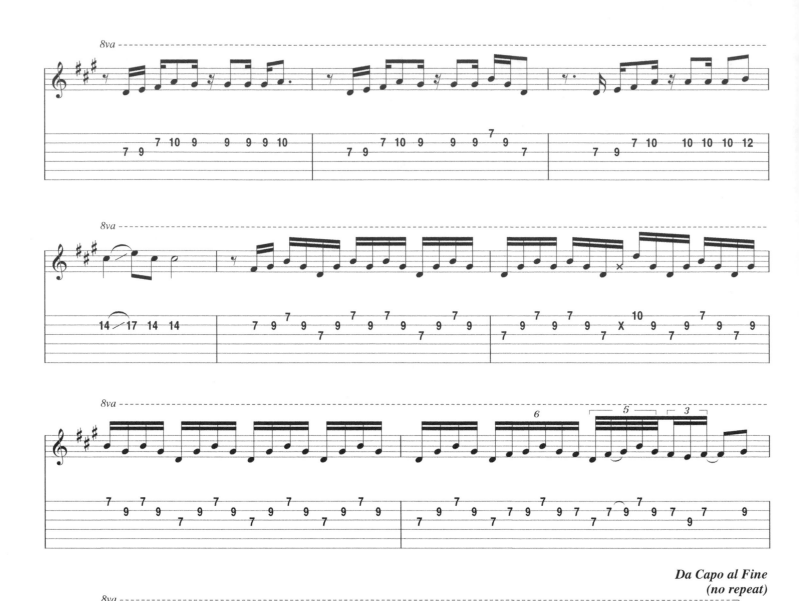

Da Capo al Fine
(no repeat)

Before moving on to our Mixolydian jam, let's learn a few licks, because…licks are cool! You can never have too many licks! These are in D Mixolydian and emphasize the major 3rd (F#) and the ♭7th (C).

6 **Fig. 17 – Mixolydian Lick 1**

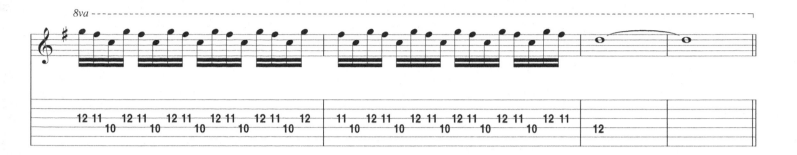

7 **Fig. 18 – Mixolydian Lick 2**

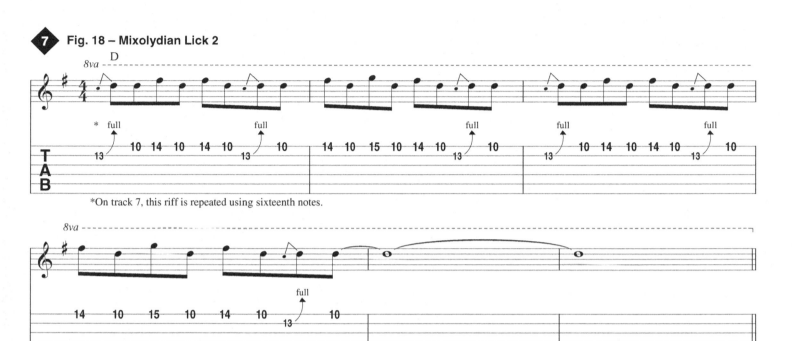

*On track 7, this riff is repeated using sixteenth notes.

Now let's try a Mixolydian jam over a droning D bass note. The bass is still just playing one note (in this case, D). The Mixolydian guitar melody is what is giving the song its modal sound.

8 **Fig. 19 – D Mixolydian Solo**

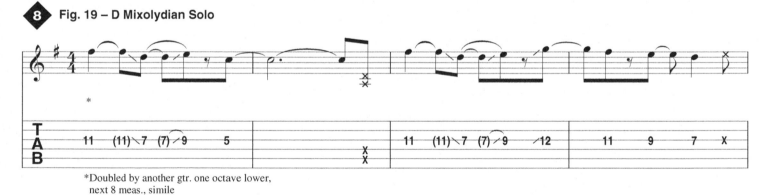

*Doubled by another gtr. one octave lower,
  next 8 meas., simile

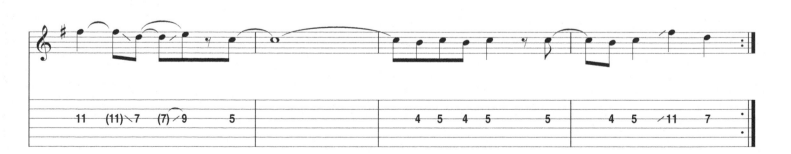

*Doubled by another gtr. one octave lower, next 4 meas., simile

**Doubled by another gtr. one octave lower, next 4 meas., simile

*Doubled by another gtr. next 4 meas., simile

*Doubled by another gtr. one octave lower, next 4 meas., simile

After listening to this solo and learning some of the licks, try jamming over the droning D bass with the D Mixolydian scale.

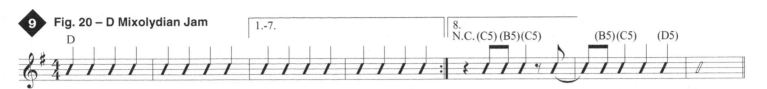

9 **Fig. 20 – D Mixolydian Jam**

Just as we used the Lydian and Mixolydian modes to spice up the solo, we can use several modes with *minor* tonalities to make things interesting as well.

The three modes used to create minor sounds are:

1. Dorian

2. Phrygian

3. Aeolian (natural minor)

When compared to the natural minor, the Dorian mode has a *raised 6th*; Phrygian is a natural minor scale with a ♭*2nd*. We'll do these with their roots on A.

A Aeolian (natural minor)	A–B–C–D–E–F–G–A
A Dorian	A–B–C–D–E–**F♯**–G–A
A Phrygian	A–**B**♭–C–D–E–F–G–A

Below are five patterns for A Dorian and five patterns for A Phrygian.

Fig. 21 – A Dorian Patterns

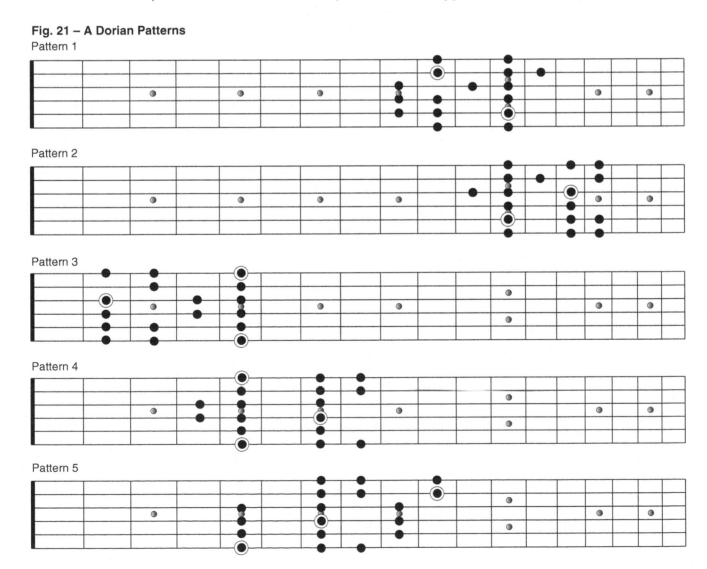

Pattern 1

Pattern 2

Pattern 3

Pattern 4

Pattern 5

Fig. 22 – A Phrygian Patterns

Pattern 1

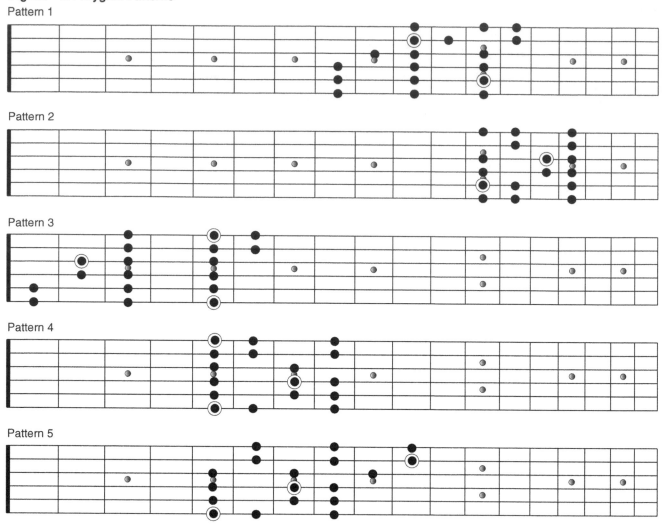

Pattern 2

Pattern 3

Pattern 4

Pattern 5

Let's start our minor jamming with some A Dorian licks. Remember: you can never have too many licks!

10 **Fig. 23 – A Dorian Licks 1 & 2**

Lick 1

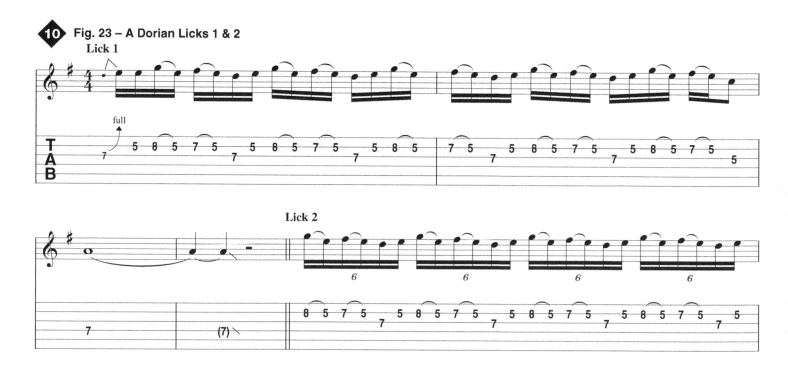

Lick 2

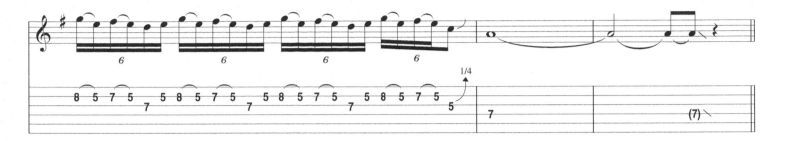

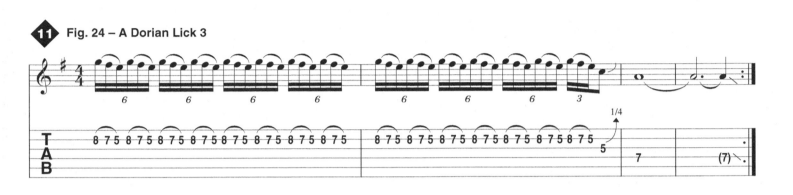

11 Fig. 24 – A Dorian Lick 3

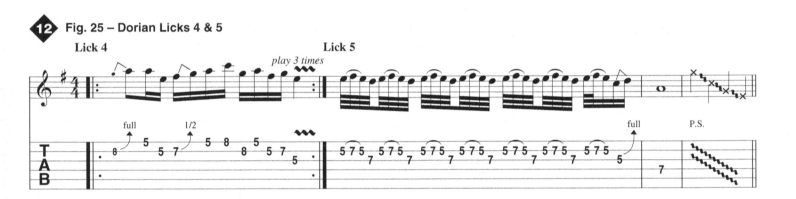

12 Fig. 25 – Dorian Licks 4 & 5

Now you can either check out the sample solo or, if you can't wait, go straight to the jam track.

13 Fig. 26 – A Dorian Solo

14 **Fig. 27 – A Dorian Jam**

Phrygian is a very "dark" sounding mode. It is defined by the half-step interval between the root and the ♭2nd. These next few licks use this to emphasize the Phrygian sound.

Fig. 28 – Phrygian Licks 1-4

Lick 1

*Doubled by another gtr. one octave lower, next 6 meas., simile.

Lick 2

Lick 3

*Doubled by another gtr. two octaves lower, next 6 meas., simile.

Lick 4

Lick 5 in Fig. 29 ends with more of a melodic harmony. Check it out.

Fig. 29 – Phrygian Licks 1, 2, & 5

*Doubled by another gtr. two octaves lower, next 10 meas., simile.

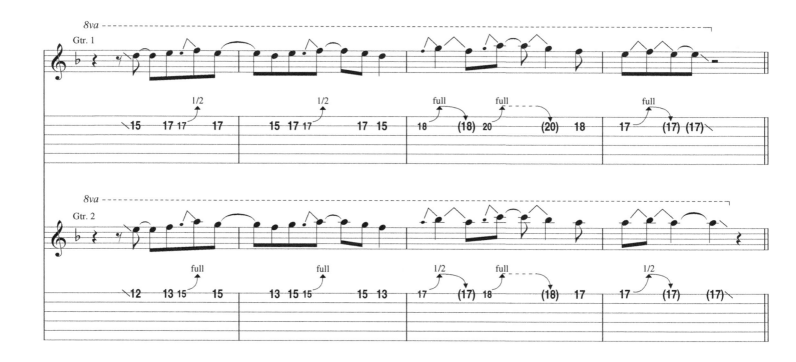

Now it's your turn. I want to hear some amazing Phrygian ideas over this static A groove. Remember: I know where you live!

17 **Fig. 30 – A Phrygian Jam**

You may have noticed we left out Ionian and Aeolian licks. This is because there are about 567,974 of those licks in our two previous books!

We've also left out the Locrian mode. This is because it is simply not used much. Have you ever tried paying your rent by jamming over a static m7♭5 chord? If you'd like to sound a little twisted, try it out. The Locrian mode is a minor scale with a ♭2 and a ♭5. Use Locrian over a diminished triad or a m7♭5 chord.

3. MODAL SONGS

Listen to the following song. Grab your guitar and find the one note that sounds like "home."

18 Fig. 31 – Southern Rock Solo

*p = pick   m = middle figner

*slide up and release bend at the same time.

Fade Out

I hope you chose D. D sounds like the "home" note and the *home note is always I* (the first note of the scale).

Now we'll find out the exact name of the key. Back in Chapter 1 you learned the order of chords in a major key:

Fig. 32

I	II	III	IV	V	VI	VII
major	minor	minor	major	major	minor	diminished

Now let's take a look at the chords of the song. There are three major chords: D, C, and G. Can you fit them into the chart above? (Hint: two of the chords are next to each other in the alphabet and are, therefore, next to each other in the chart.)

That's right! C and D are next to each other in the alphabet and would fit where C is IV, D is V, and G is I.

Fig. 33

I	II	III	IV	V	VI	VII
G major	A minor	B minor	C major	D major	E minor	F# diminished

So, in theory, this song is from the key of G major. But remember, your ear said that D is the home and home is always I. *That means the key is a G major scale that starts on D.*

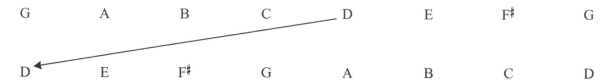

What's the name?...*D Mixolydian.*

Fig. 34

I	II	III	IV	V	VI	VII
D major	E minor	F# diminished	G major	A minor	B minor	C major

We've done enough talking; let's do some playing! We'll use G major scales for soloing—but remember: *G isn't the cool note anymore—D is!* Try hitting a lot of Ds—especially when you end your phrases. Most of my solo was from this position:

Fig. 35
G Major Pattern 1 / D Mixolydian Pattern 3

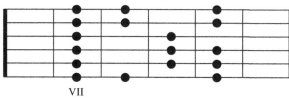

VII

Have fun playing with the track; then you can learn some of my Mixolydian licks from the solo.

19 Fig. 36

Here's another one. First listen to track 20, then try to figure out the answers.

20 Fig. 37

22

Ear answer: _____ is home.

Theory answer: _____ is home.

Final answer: _____

Answers: Ear—G is home; Theory—B♭ major scale; Final—G Aeolian.

Now check out what I did over the progression in Fig. 37:

21 **Fig. 38 – G Aeolian Solo**

23

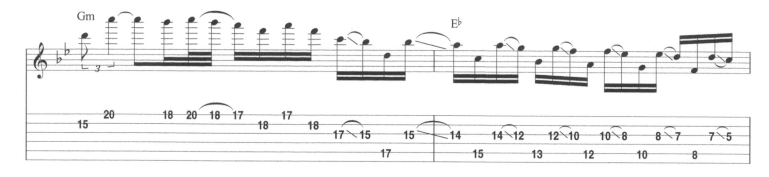

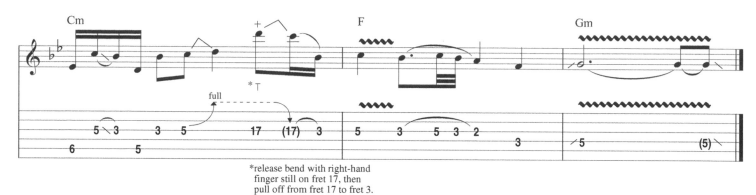

*release bend with right-hand
finger still on fret 17, then
pull off from fret 17 to fret 3.

You'll notice I use a lot of minor pentatonic sounds in this solo. Does that mean I'm not playing Aeolian? No. The minor pentatonic scale is just a smaller version of the Aeolian scale—look!

G Aeolian:	G	A	B♭	C	D	E♭	F
G minor pentatonic:	G		B♭	C	D		F

Here's one that has that "Satch" sound. (hint: consider the B/A as a B major chord when analyzing. The "A" is for the bass player.) Danny and I will trade leads on this one so you can hear our different approaches to modal playing. The first solo is a very linear solo (meaning that the notes are played consecutively from the scale shapes). Also, it's very technically demanding.[2]

The second solo uses a lot of double stops to contrast with the diarrhea-hand noodlings of my partner. Also, you'll notice I played a lot more melodically than he did…geez!

Fig. 39 – Satch Solo

Section 1

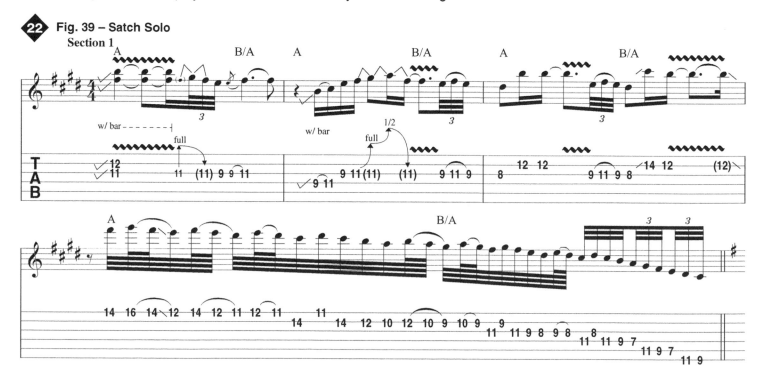

[2] For a more in-depth look at the techniques needed to pull this solo off, check out *Rock Lead Guitar Techniques*.

*Note fretted while string is still bent.

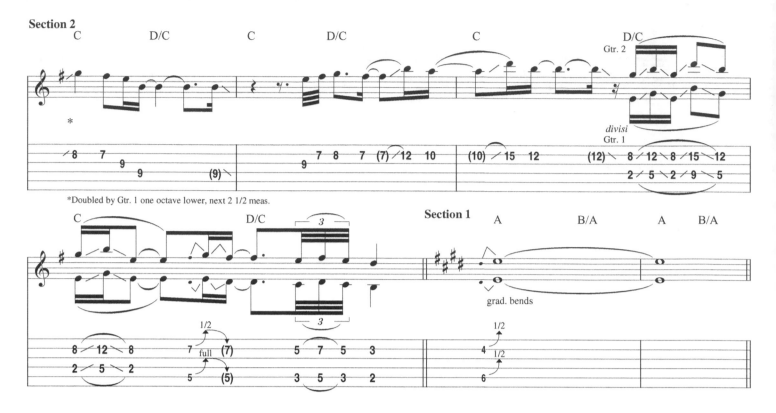

*Doubled by Gtr. 1 one octave lower, next 2 1/2 meas.

Answer the following questions about Fig. 39.

Section 1

Ear answer: _____ is home.

Theory answer: _____ is home.

Final answer: _____

Answers: Ear—A is home;
Theory—E major scale;
Final—A Lydian

Section 2

Ear answer: _____ is home.

Theory answer: _____ is home.

Final answer: _____

Answers: Ear—C is home;
Theory—G is home;
Final—C Lydian

Now let's turn the heat up a notch and delve into some more advanced chords—the seventh chords. They were listed in Chapter 1, but here they are again, as they fall into the harmonized major scale.

Fig. 40

I	II	III	IV	V	VI	VII
major 7	minor 7	minor 7	major 7	dominant 7	minor 7	minor 7♭5

Figure out a mode for the following song. (Hint: there's only one dominant chord in a key—it's always V).

23 **Fig. 41 – G7 Funk Solo**

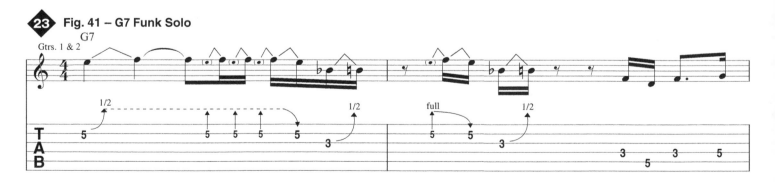

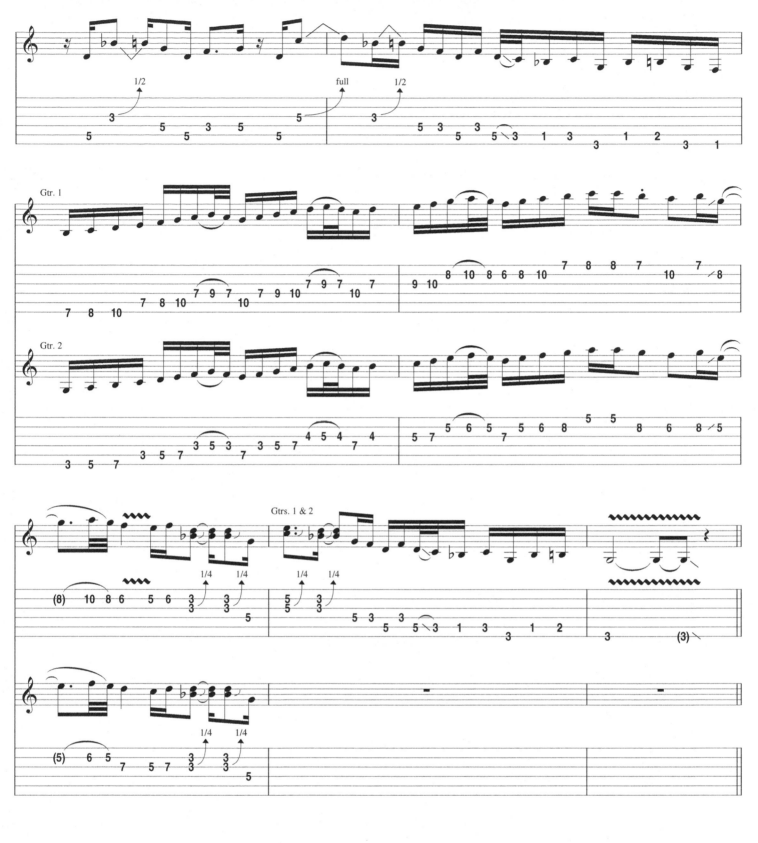

Ear answer: _____ is home.

Theory answer: _____ is home.

Final answer: _____

Answers: Ear—G is home; Theory—C major scale; Final—G Mixolydian.

Look again at my solo in Fig. 41. The first four measures are played in third position in what we would call "G minor pentatonic." But look closer at the music. You'll notice that every time I hit a B♭, I bend it upwards towards a B♮. This gives the scale more of a major sound, and actually makes it a great substitute for

Mixolydian. Check it out:

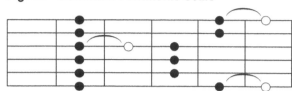

| G Mixolydian: | G | | A | | B | | C | | D | | E | | F |
| G minor pentatonic with raised 3rds | G | | | B♭ B bend | | | C | | D | | | | F |

What should we call this scale? How about the *Dominant Pentatonic* scale.

Fig. 42 – Dominant Pentatonic Scale

Now it's your turn to solo.

24 **Fig. 43 – G Mixolydian Jam**

G7

play 5 times

Here's one that has a Santana-type feel.

25 **Fig. 44 – Solo à la Carlos**

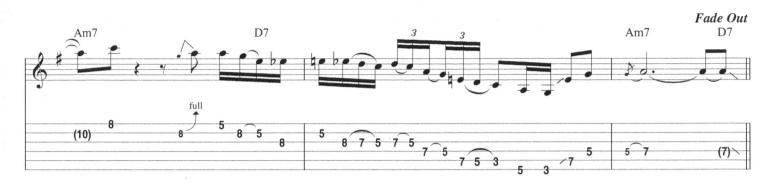

Ear answer: _____ is home.

Theory answer: _____ is home.

Final answer: _____ _____

Answers: Ear—A is home; Theory—G major scale; Final—A Dorian.

Now look at the solo I played— I did it again! I played in a pentatonic position for the majority of this solo. You must be thinking, "I thought the name of this chapter was 'modal playing,' not 'pentatonic scales.'"

What I'm trying to show you here is that modes really aren't that uncommon. A lot of the music you've been listening to your whole life uses modes. The most natural way I know of playing them is in reference to our good ol' buddy—the pentatonic scale. Take a look:

On any major mode you can use a major pentatonic scale.

A major pentatonic:	A	B	C#		E	F#		A
A major:	A	B	C#	D	E	F#	G#	A
A Lydian:	A	B	C#	D#	E	F#	G#	A
A Mixolydian:	A	B	C#	D	E	F#	G	A

On any minor mode you can use a minor pentatonic scale.

A minor pentatonic:	A		C	D	E		G	A
A Dorian:	A	B	C	D	E	F#	G	A
A Phrygian:	A	Bb	C	D	E	F	G	A
A Aeolian:	A	B	C	D	E	F	G	A

In performance, I'll blend whatever scale I'm working with together with its corresponding pentatonic scale. For A Dorian, I'll play a little A minor pentatonic, then use some A Dorian, and then go back to A minor pentatonic. It makes for a very natural sounding solo. Now, let's see what you can "blend" as you jam over Fig. 45 (track 26).

26 **Fig. 45**

*stay on Am7 last time

This next tune uses the Mixolydian mode in two keys: D and A.

27 **Fig. 46 – D and A Mixolydian Solo**

Drop D Tuning:
① = E   ④ = D
② = B   ⑤ = A
③ = G   ⑥ = D

*Key signatures in this fig. reflect the scale being used, and don't necessarily correspond to the overall key of the song.

Like we did earlier, let's combine a couple of different modes on one progression. Follow along closely to track 28 and then try the jam track (track 29).

Fig. 47 – Modal Solo

*key signatures in this fig. reflect the scale
being used, and don't necessarily correspond
to the overall key of the song.

**played ahead of the beat

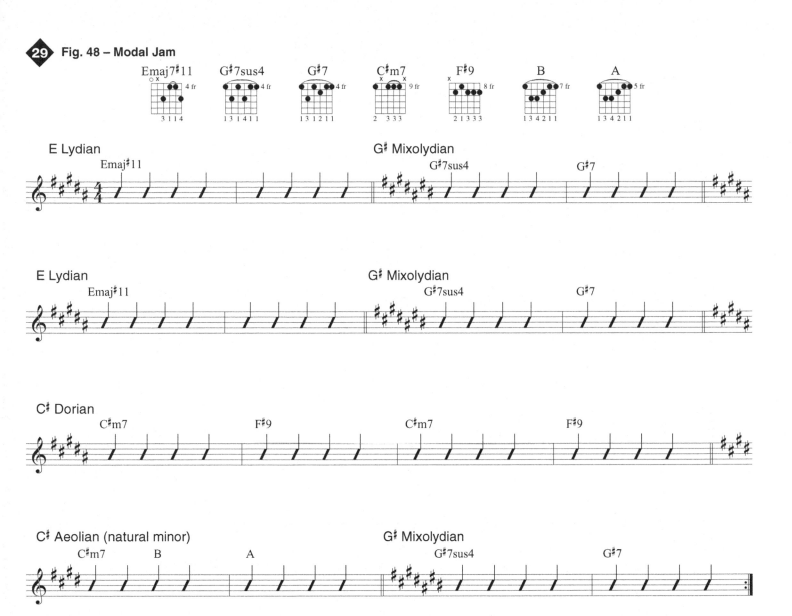

CHAPTER 3
COVERING CHORDS

DOUBLE STOPS

A *double stop* is when two notes are played simultaneously. We've been using them throughout the book, but let's take a formal look at them now. Common double stops include 3rds, 4ths, 5ths, 6ths, and octaves. Double stops work well as fills and as a melodic tool to help locate chord tones. Below are five exercises designed to familiarize you with each of these interval shapes.

Here is the G major scale harmonized in 3rds:

Fig. 49 – G Major Scale Harmonized in Thirds

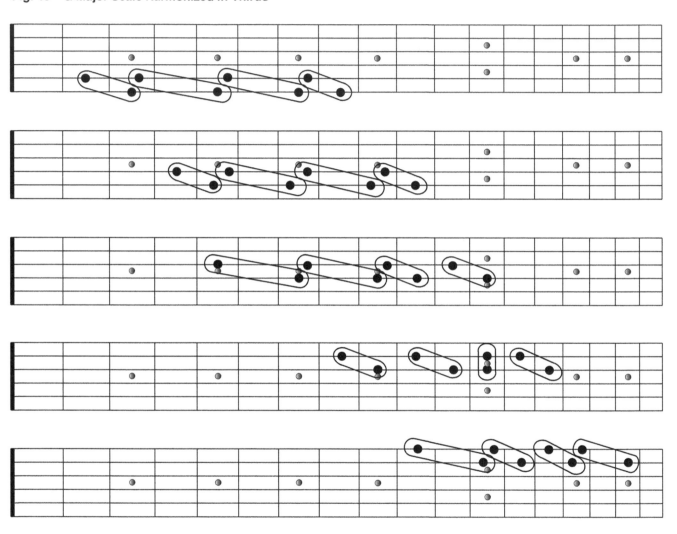

Although it is possible to play 4ths and 5ths with the diatonic scale, the five-note pentatonic scale works well for these double stops because it focuses on the strong notes of the scale. These double stops are written in E major pentatonic.

Fig. 50 – E Major Pentatonic Sacle in Fourths

*Although E-G♯ is a major 3rd, I've included it in order to stay within the major pentatonic.

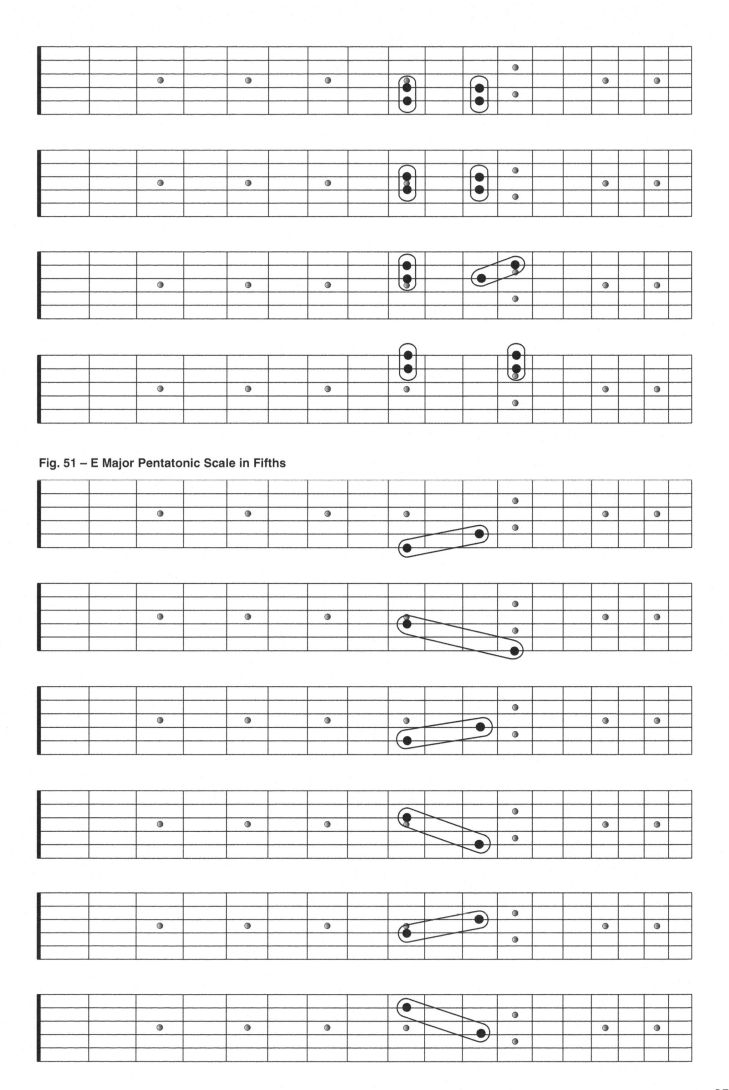

Fig. 51 – E Major Pentatonic Scale in Fifths

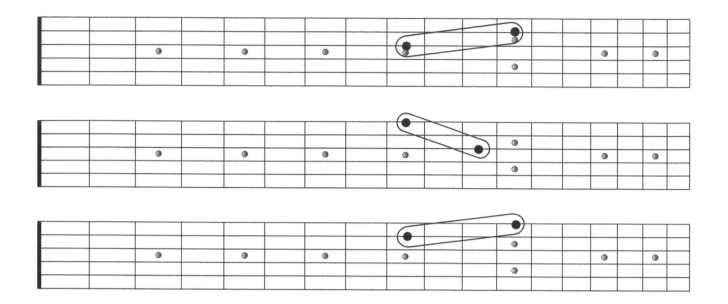

Try these with all five pentatonic patterns.[3]

Sixths work well when played up the fretboard, rather than in one position.

Fig. 52 – G Major Scale in Sixths

If you're feeling brave, try them in one position.

Fig. 53 – G Major in Sixths (one position)

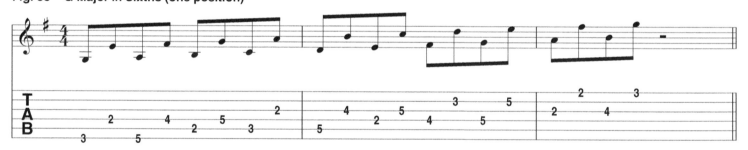

Let's put some of these ideas to use. Note in the transcription which type of double stop is used.

30 **Fig. 54 – Double Stops**

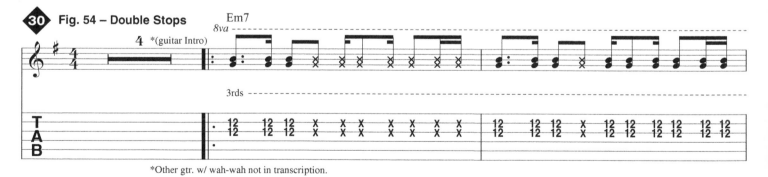

*Other gtr. w/ wah-wah not in transcription.

---

[3] The five pentatonic patterns were presendted in our first book, *Rock Lead Basics.*

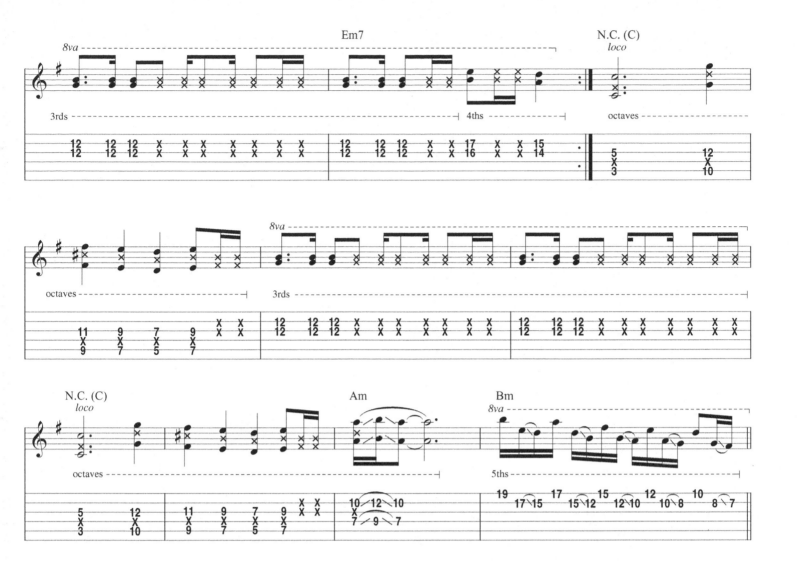

CHORD RIFFS

Some of my favorite double-stop ideas are based on chord shapes. The idea is simple: while holding down a chord shape, add a scale tone. The result will be two notes ringing simultaneously—a double stop. In the following diagrams, the solid dots represent a chord shape while the X's indicate scale tones which can be added to the chord.

Fig. 55 – Major Chords

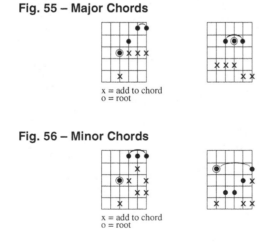

x = add to chord
o = root

Fig. 56 – Minor Chords

x = add to chord
o = root

Now let's try using some of these double stops in a musical situation.

*Accompaniment gtr. not notated in transcription.

COVERING THE CHORDS

In our experience, we've found that most rock songs fit into one of two different categories: a "drone progression" or a "changing progression."

A *drone progression* is when the tonic of the key literally drones throughout the progression. The progression below is a classic example of a drone progression. In fact, I put a keyboard track on there to point out the drone.

32 **Fig. 58 – Drone Progression**

These progressions rely on the vocal melody or, in our case, the guitar solo to hold the audience's interest because there's so little action coming from the chords. Therefore, to make an amazing solo on a drone progression, you'll need a lot of variety and strong musical statements to make up for the lack of variety in the chords.[4]

A *changing progression* is one where it doesn't feel as comfortable to drone throughout—it seems that the drone would like to shift for certain chords. This is a progression begging to be followed. Now, the progression is the leader and the guitarist is the follower.

33 **Fig. 59 – Changing Progression**

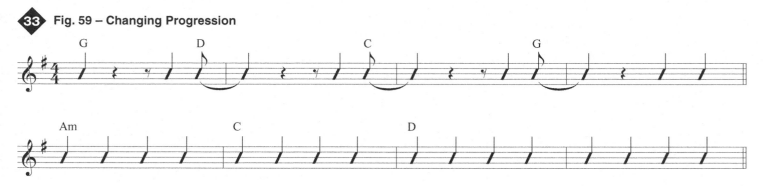

To be successful at playing changes, you should first learns how to cover each chord. For instance, when the band plays a G chord, you play G–B–D (notes of the chord). Now, some of you may think it's time to pull out those arpeggios you've been practicing. Yes—arpeggios are good—but often sound uninspired and even predictable when soloing. Instead, I'm going to teach you three-string triad shapes. Learn the six major shapes and six minor shapes in the following figure. They are all rooted on G.

Fig. 60 – Major and Minor Triad Shapes

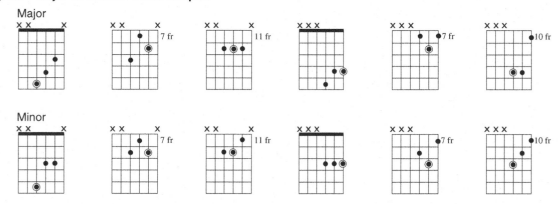

Here's an example of how to work with these triad shapes.

34 **Fig. 61 – Covering Chords (Solo 1)**

---

[4] For more on this subject, refer to *Rock Lead Guitar Techniques*, where the phrasing concepts are explained in more depth.

Expanding the Triad

After you've nailed the triads, let's take things a step further. This time, using the same triad shapes, throw in some extra notes (without lifting your fingers off the triad). We could talk theory about which notes to add, but I think you should just wing it and have fun. Try these out over the jam track (track 36).

35 Fig. 62 – Covering Chords (Solo 2)

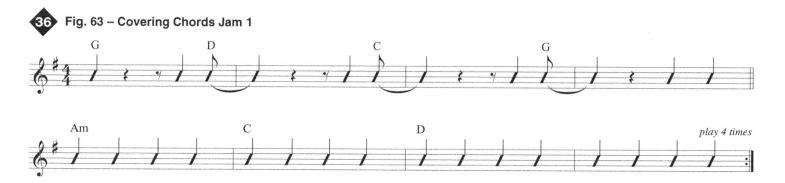

Adding Pentatonics

By now you should be getting used to playing chord tones. Next, we'll add a pentatonic scale for every chord.

The exercise works like this:

1. First, hit chord tones.

2. Expand a bit with extra notes.

3. Then play a lick out of the pentatonic scale. For a G major chord, use the G major pentatonic scale; for a D major chord, use the D major pentatonic scale; for an A minor chord, use the A minor pentatonic scale; and so on.

Since there's so much to do, we'll double the length of every chord. Use Fig. 65 (track 38) for practicing, and I'll show you how in Fig. 64 (track 37).

37 Fig. 64 – Covering Chords (Solo 3)

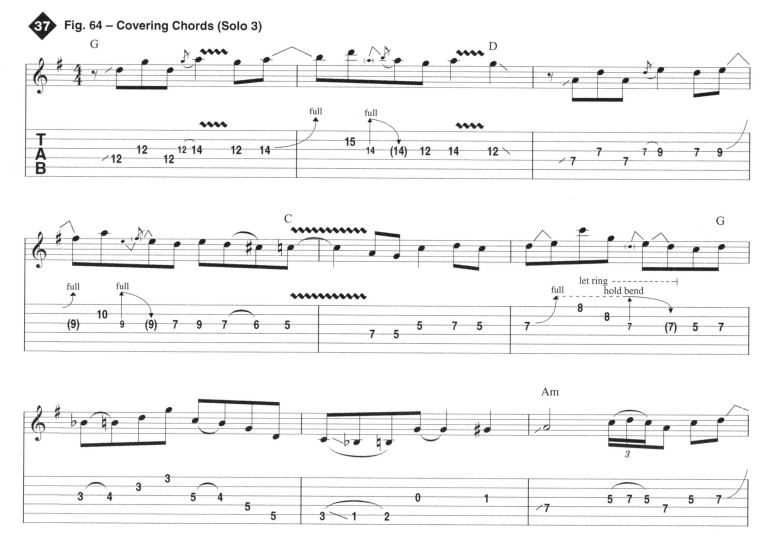

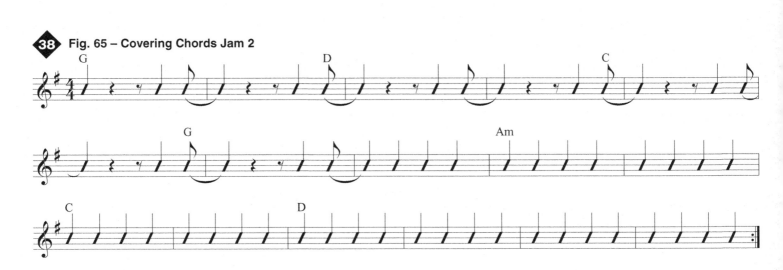

38 Fig. 65 – Covering Chords Jam 2

I can't say enough how important the above exercise is for anyone who wants to cover chord changes. It should become part of your routine for the next several months. Now that you've got a handle on the chord tones, I'll give you some licks based on chord tone thinking.

39 Fig. 66 – Chord Tone Licks

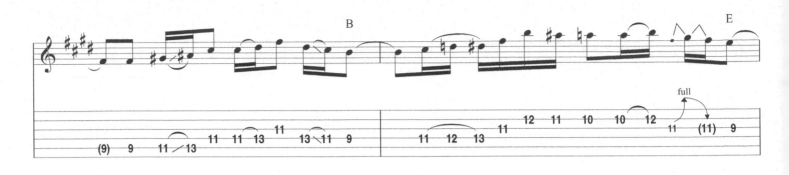

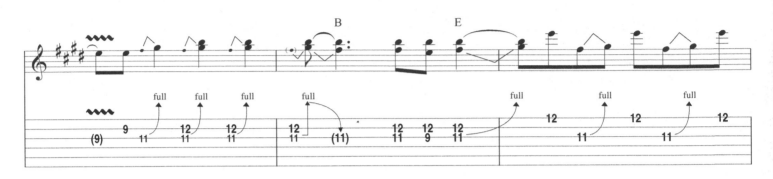

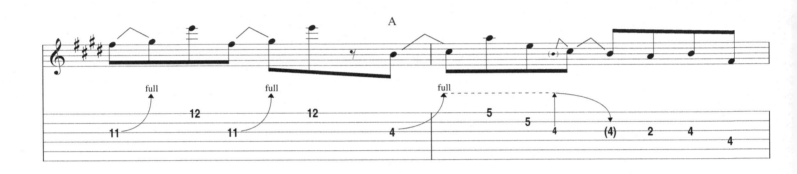

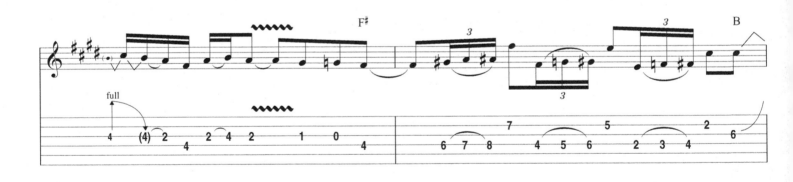

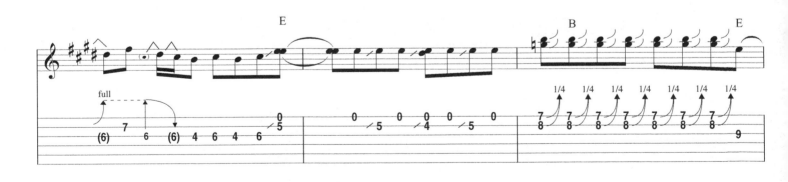

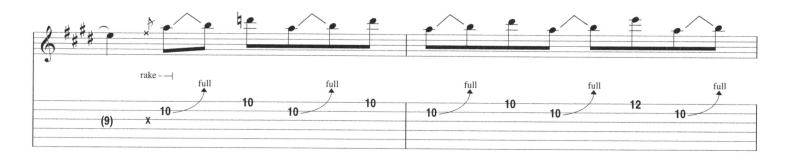

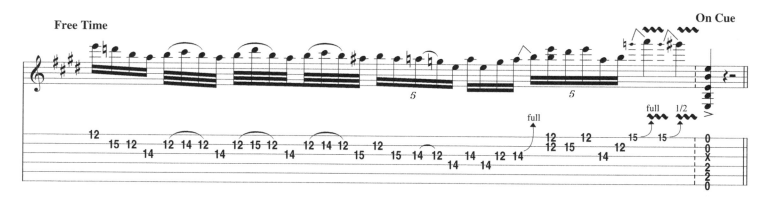

CHAPTER 4
SOLOING OVER CHANGES

THE HARMONIC MINOR SCALE

At this point in the book, you may be asking yourself "why do we need *another* minor scale?" After all, we've already studied the Aeolian, Dorian, and Phrygian modes —all minor scales. Good question; glad you asked. Play these two progressions:

Fig. 67

Progression 1

| Am | Dm | Em | Am |

Progression 2

| Am | Dm | E | Am |

Using your ear as your guide, which progression seems to have the greatest impact? Hopefully you can hear that the E major chord in the second progression has a stronger resolution back to the A minor chord:

Fig. 68   Em   Am   E   Am

Because this type of a chord progression is so common and so powerful, a scale was created that would allow us to play over the major V chord in a minor progression. The result is the *harmonic minor* scale.

The harmonic minor scale is a natural minor scale with a raised 7th. Here's a comparison of A natural minor with A harmonic minor:

A minor:	A–B–C–D–E–F–G–A
A Harmonic Minor:	A–B–C–D–E–F–**G**♯–A

As you play through the following patterns, try to visualize the harmonic minor scale as a natural minor scale with one note altered. (The 7th is raised a half step.) This is easier than memorizing an entirely new set of scales.

Fig. 69   A Aeolian   A Harmonic Minor

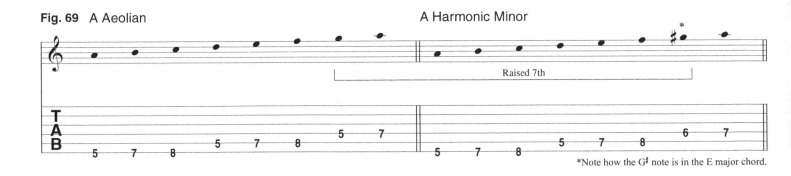

*Note how the G♯ note is in the E major chord.

Fig. 70 – A Harmonic Minor (cont'd)

Pattern 1

Pattern 2

Pattern 3

Pattern 4

Pattern 5

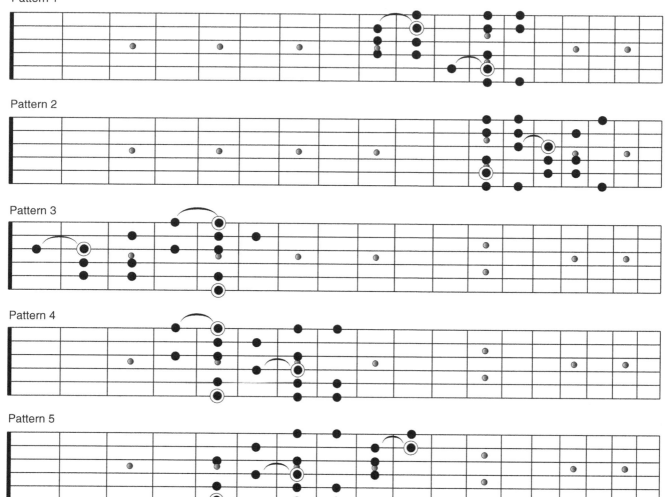

The three-note-per-string patterns are also very useful:

Fig. 71 – Three-Note-Per-String Patterns

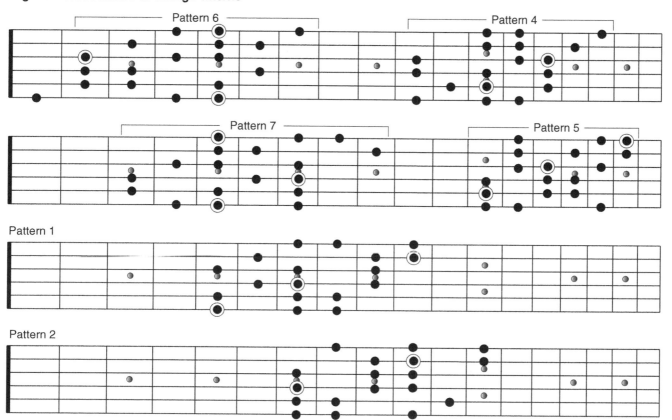

Pattern 3

As we have done previously with the major scale, it is also possible to build chords from the harmonic minor scale. Let's take a look at the chords of the harmonized harmonic minor scale:

Fig. 72 – Harmonized Harmonic Minor Scale

I	II	III	IV	V	VI	VII
minor	diminished	augmented	minor	major	major	diminished

Chord Types for A Harmonic Minor

Fig. 73 – Harmonic Minor Scale Harmonized with Seventh Chords

I	II	III	IV	V	VI	VII
m(maj7)	m7♭5	maj7♯5	m7	7	maj7	°7

Chord Types for A Harmonic Minor

One of the most important things to remember out of all of this information is: *the harmonic minor scale works well over the V chord in a minor key if the V chord is a major triad or a dominant chord.* Memorize it! This is the main reason the scale was created in the first place!

Try out this new scale over the following progression. Remember—only use the harmonic minor over the major V chord.

40 **Fig. 74 – Harmonic Minor Jam 1**

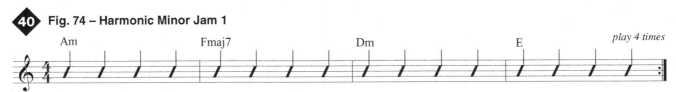

Let's try one with some seventh chords. Pretend you're jamming at a party with some friends and they say "go for it!," over these chords:

41 **Fig. 75 – Harmonic Minor Jam 2**

What would you do? Panic? I hope not! By now you should be able to recognize that the key center is C minor. So, do you play C natural minor over all of the chords? No, no, no—you'd be missing out on all the fun stuff! Notice the G7 chord? That's right—it's a dominant V chord in a minor key, so play *C harmonic minor* over G7.

Check out the solo (Fig. 75) and then try one yourself over Fig. 75.

42 Fig. 76 – Harmonic Minor Solo

*played ahead of the beat

THE DIMINISHED SEVENTH CHORD

Another useful application of the harmonic minor scale is with the diminished seventh chord. In a minor key, the diminished seventh chord (VII) functions much like the dominant seventh chord (V). It sets up a strong resolution back to the I chord, or serves as a passing chord to other chords in the key. In fact, the VII chord can be used along with the V chord or as a substitute for the V chord. I'll show you what I mean. Play this next progression:

43 Fig. 77

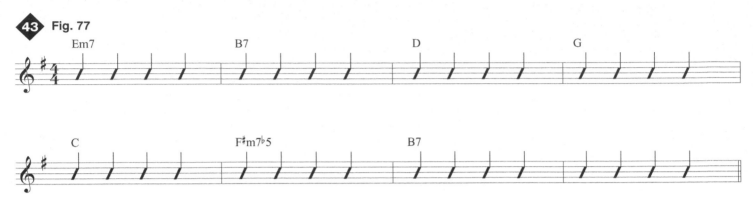

By now you should know that the B7 chord is from the E harmonic minor scale (it's the V chord). Let's try substituting the VII chord (D#°7) for B7 in the following example:

44 Fig. 78 – Solo with a Diminished Seventh Chord

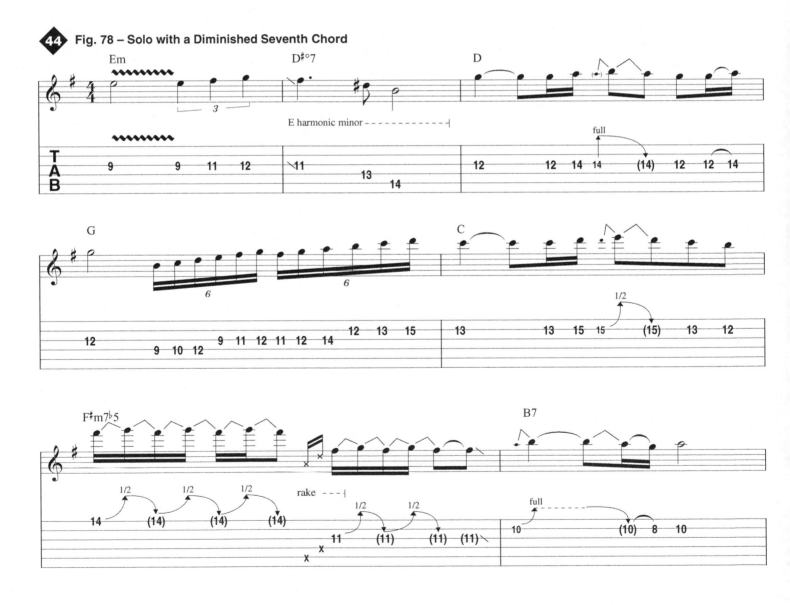

50

Did you notice that the D#"7 chord has better voice leading (it sounds smoother) into the D major chord than the B7 chord? When you write a hit song with this stuff, don't forget to cut me in on my 10%! Now you try it!

45 Fig. 79 – Jam with a Diminished Seventh Chord

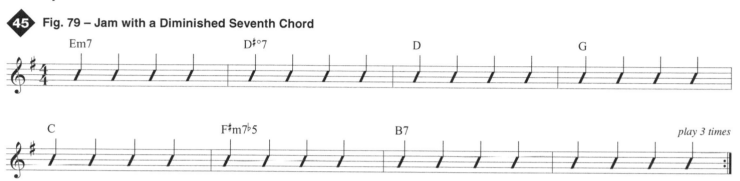

THE DIMINISHED SEVENTH ARPEGGIO

The diminished seventh arpeggio can be used anywhere the diminished seventh chord is used. Why?—because the arpeggio is simply the notes of the chord played in the form of a scale. Below are two patterns of the diminished seventh arpeggio.

Fig. 80 – G# Diminished Seventh Arpeggio

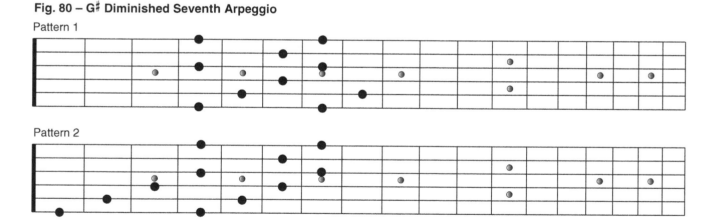

SYMMETRICAL SHAPES

The diminished seventh chord and the diminished seventh arpeggio are known as symmetrical patterns. This means that if we play a diminished seventh chord or arpeggio we can play the same shape every three frets and it will be *exactly the same!* The chord will simply be an inversion of itself each time you climb the fretboard. To try this out, take a diminished seventh chord and, without rearranging your fingers, simply slide the chord up or down three frets. The chord will function in exactly the same way; it will now be an inversion of itself. If we slide up four times we're back to where we started, one octave higher. This is a great way to play something that only sounds difficult.

Fig. 81 – Diminished Arpeggio Symetrical Shapes

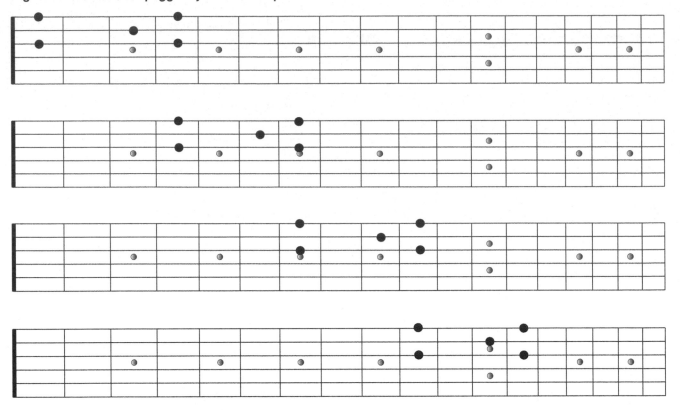

Fig. 82 – Diminished Chord Symetrical Shapes

THE DARK SIDE OF HARMONIC MINOR

Another common place to use the harmonic minor scale is when you have two major triads 1/2 step apart.

If we look at Fig. 82 we see that this is a V–VI progression in the key of B harmonic minor. The V and the VI is the only place where we have two major triads 1/2 step apart.

But wait—there's more!…

For those of you who would really like to impress your friends and neighbors, the fifth mode of the harmonic minor scale is called *Phrygian Dominant*. This means that *F♯ Phrygian dominant has the same notes as B harmonic minor.*

I think we're ready for some licks. You may notice some similarities between this sound and a certain Swedish guitarist popular in the eighties. History buffs may want to look back a bit further to a certain German guitarist from the late seventies. If you can't figure out who I'm talking about, their initials are Y.M. and U.R., respectively.

46 Fig. 84 – F♯ Phrygian Dominant Riff 1

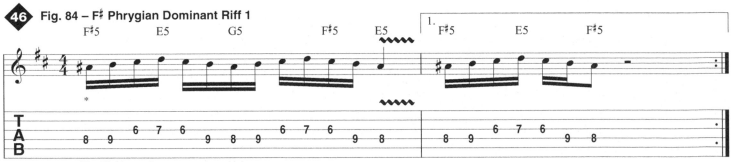

*Doubled by another gtr. one octave higher.

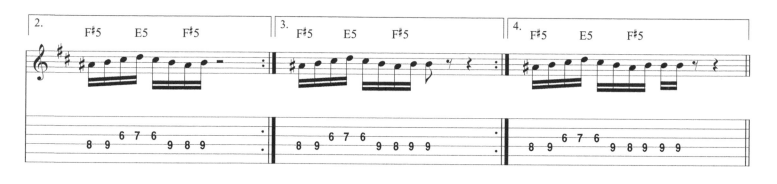

47 **Fig. 85 – F♯ Phrygian Dominant Riff 2**

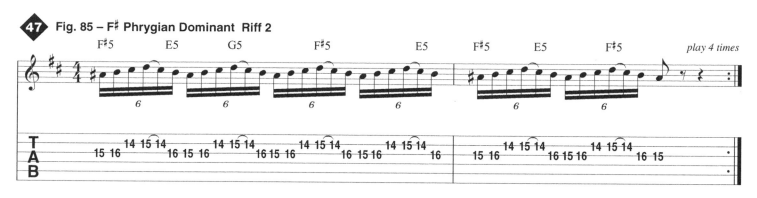

48 **Fig. 86 – F♯ Phrygian Dominant Riff 1, 3 & 4**

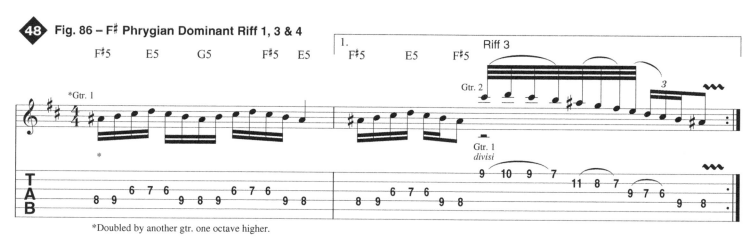

*Doubled by another gtr. one octave higher.

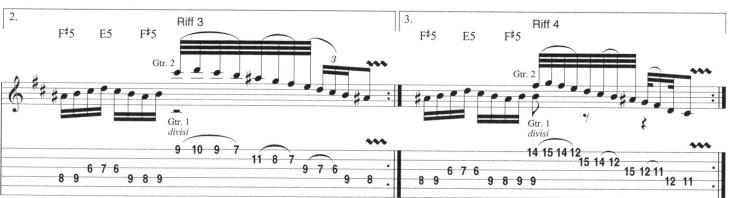

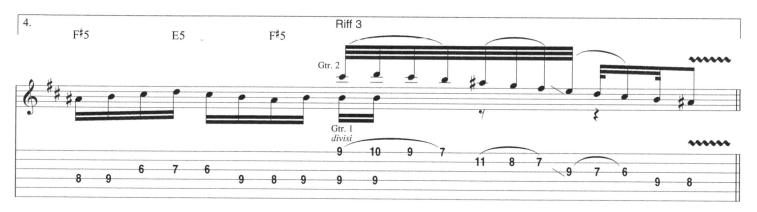

Now have some fun and experiment with the F# Phrygian dominant scale (B harmonic minor) over Fig. 85.

49 Fig. 87 – F# Phrygian Dominant Jam

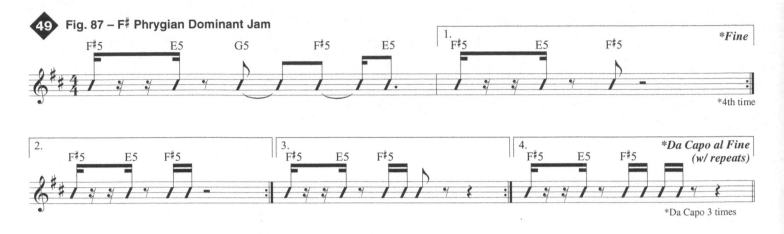

THE BLUESY HARMONIC MINOR

As you've seen, the harmonic minor scale is a great one. But sometimes, due to the style of the song, it can sound a bit "classical" or serious—especially in blues-based situation.

Have no fear! We have an answer for you: the dominant blues scale.

First of all, a blues scale is a minor pentatonic scale with the addition of a ♭5 (or #4): 1–♭3–4–♭5–5–♭7.

Fig. 88 – Blues Scale (Pattern 4)

This is the scale of choice for many players on blues-based progressions. Try the following lick and you'll see what I mean.

50 Fig. 89 – E Minor Blues Lick

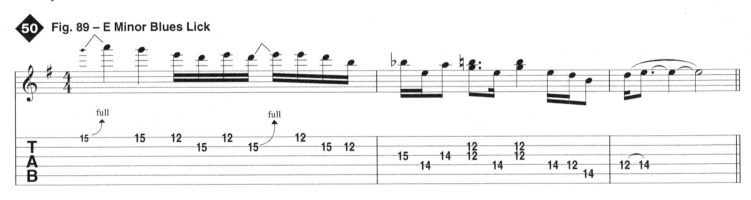

Now here's where the word "dominant" comes in. Let's take that same scale, but *every* time we hit a minor third, we'll raise it up to a major third by either bending it, hammering on to it, or sliding into it. (Remember—back in the modes chapter we touched on this.)

51 Fig. 90 – E Dominant Blues Lick

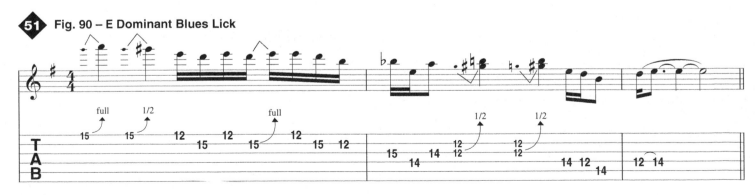

54

Blues Scale with Major Thirds

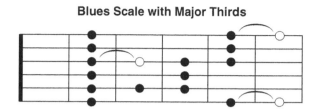

Did you notice the difference? Now the scale contains these intervals: 1–♭3 (bent up to) **3**–4–♭**5**–**5**–♭**7** (the notes of a dominant seventh chord are in bold text). See how it fits?

Now let's go back to harmonic minor. Following is a progression that uses A harmonic minor (over the E7 chord). However, the bass player is playing a little bit funky, and the regular harmonic minor might sound too square. So instead of playing A harmonic minor over E7, we'll play the E dominant blues scale. Look how many notes are in common?

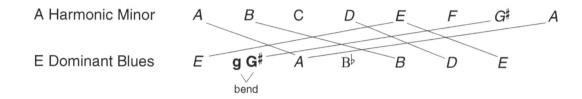

A Harmonic Minor   A   B   C   D   E   F   G♯   A

E Dominant Blues   E   **g G♯**   A   B♭   B   D   E

bend

52 Fig. 91 – "Motel California" Solo

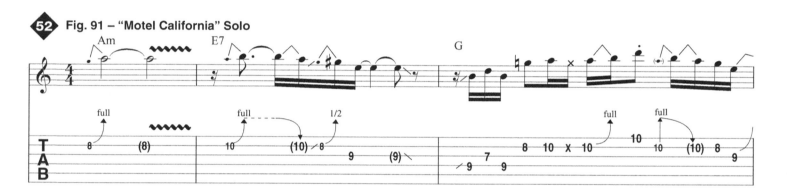

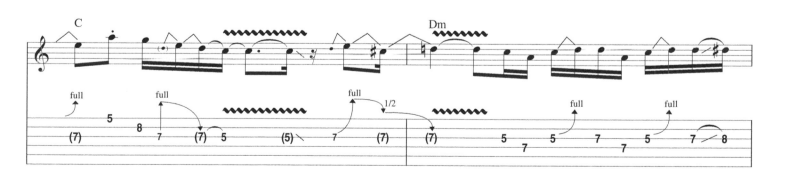

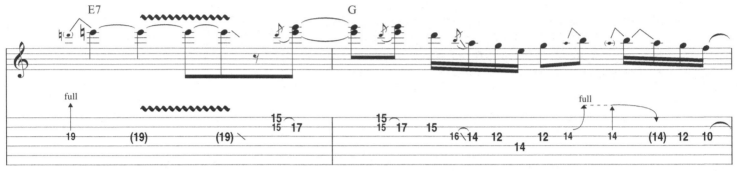

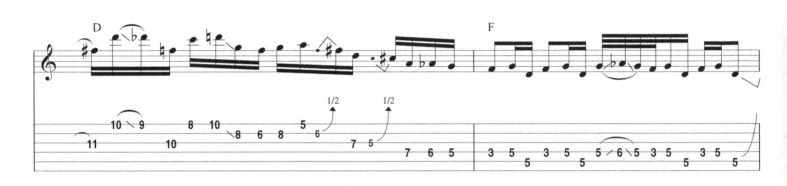

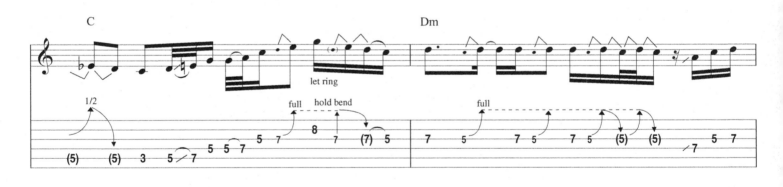

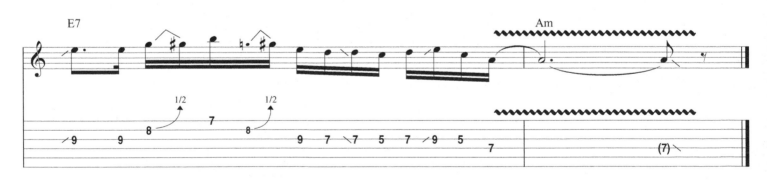

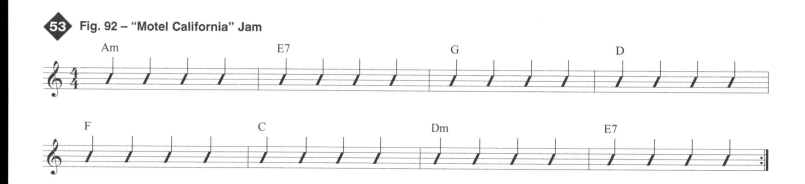

53 Fig. 92 – "Motel California" Jam

Phrasing advice: look for the *harmonic minor note* (G♯) on the E7 chords. Notice how cool it sounds to play the dominant pentatonic here.

Also, pay close attention to how every chord has been covered. This is a changing progression, not a drone progression. Look back at Chapter 3 if you skipped it. You'll learn how to cover the changes there.

One last word: don't try to play really fast on this one. *Take your time.*

MODULATIONS

A *modulation* is when a chord progression moves to another key. Take a look at the following progression:

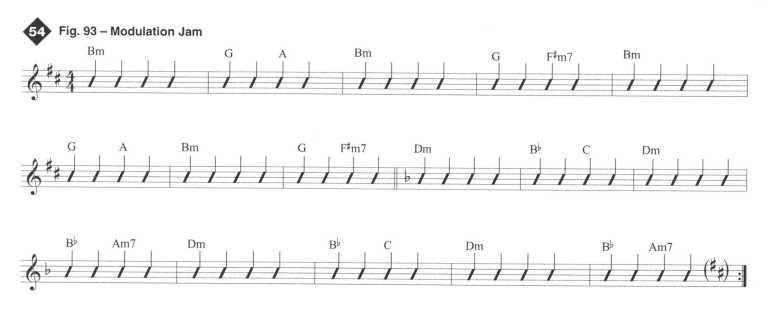

54 Fig. 93 – Modulation Jam

The first eight measures are in the key of B minor. The next eight measure modulate up a minor third (three frets) to D minor. We're going to talk about four ways to solo over a modulating chord progression.

1. *Move with the chords.* This is the most obvious way to solo over the changes. Simply take a lick and move it up a minor third (or to wherever the modulation takes you).

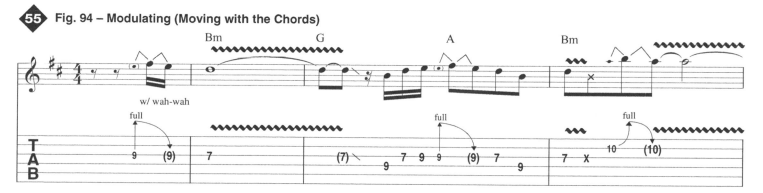

55 Fig. 94 – Modulating (Moving with the Chords)

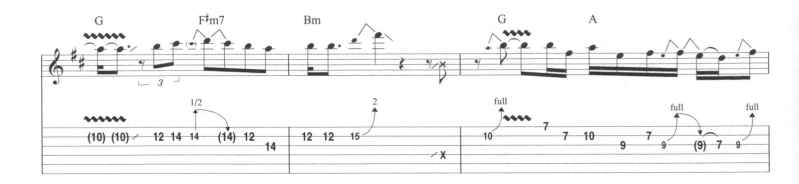

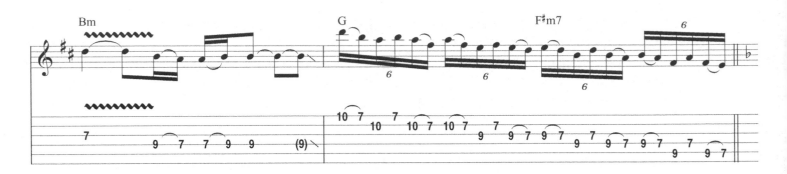

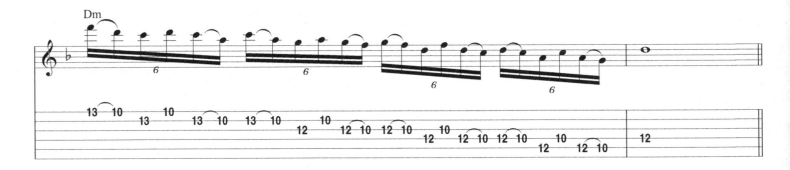

2. *Common tones.* Try holding a note that is common to both keys as the chords move underneath you. Let's compare B minor and D minor.

B minor	B–C♯–D–E–F♯–G–A
D minor	D–E–F–G–A–B♭–C

The common tones are: D, E, G, and A. D is the strongest of these because it is a chord tone of both B minor and D minor.

56 Fig. 95 – Modulating (Common Tones)

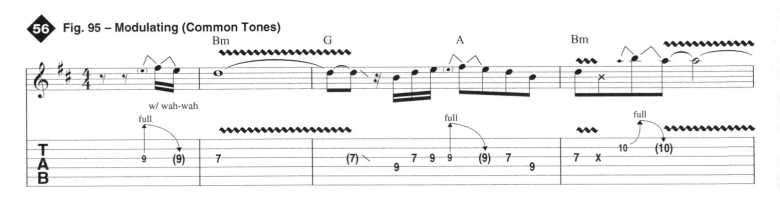

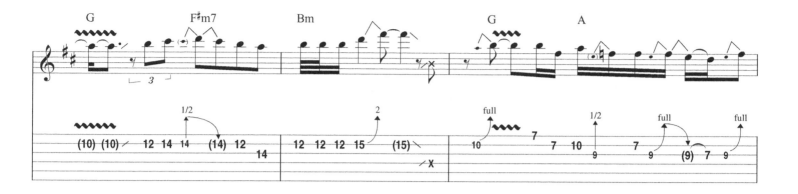

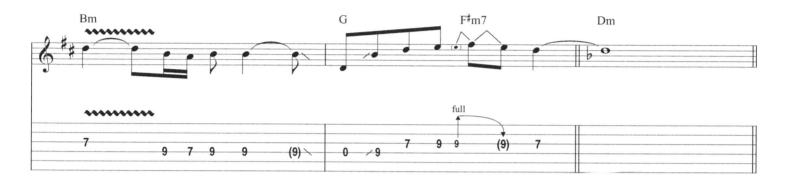

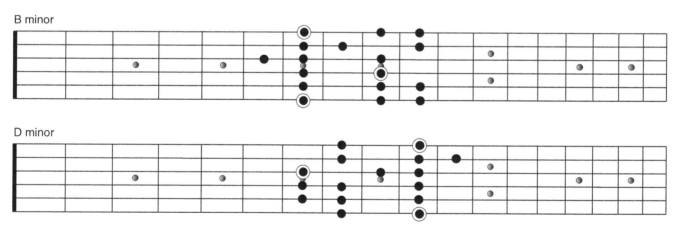

3. *Stay in one position.* If you've done your homework, you should be able to stay in one position anywhere on the neck and switch keys. This requires you to be very familiar with all of the diatonic scale patterns. Here's one possible position for this:

Fig. 96 – Modulating (Staying in One Position)

B minor

D minor

4. *Switch keys early.* If you switch keys before the modulation occurs, your solo will sound "outside" for a moment and the "resolved" when the new key arrives. A good place to start is by switching keys two beats early.

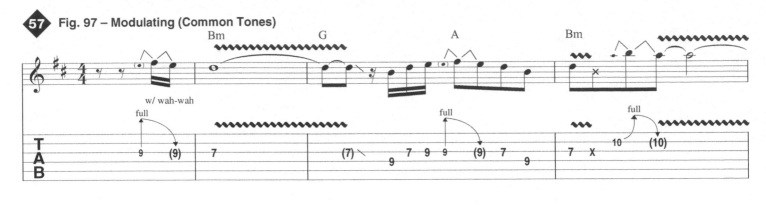

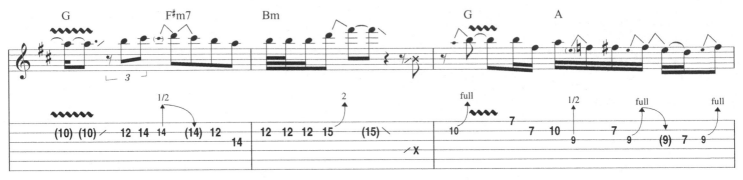

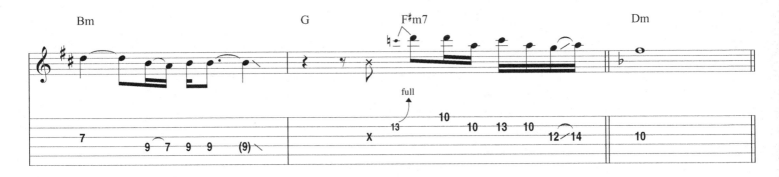

Now it's your turn. Go back to Fig. 92 (track 54) and try out your new modulation chops!

Here's another modulating progression to practice soloing over. This one switches between three keys.

58 **Fig. 98**

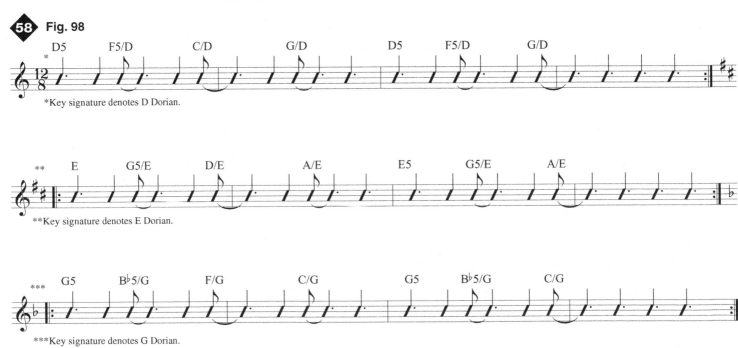

*Key signature denotes D Dorian.

**Key signature denotes E Dorian.

***Key signature denotes G Dorian.

MODAL INTERCHANGE

Listen to track 59. It sounds like a tune in E, right? Well, actually it's a tune from two different E scales: E major and E minor. This is called modal interchange. Modal interchange means using two different modes to make one song. Most commonly the major (Ionian) mode and the minor (Aeolian) mode are used.

Take a look at the chords in the harmonized E major scale and the chords of the harmonized E minor scale.

Fig. 99

E major

I	II	III	IV	V	VI	VII
E	F♯m	G♯m	A	B	C♯m	D♯°

E minor

I	II	III	IV	V	VI	VII
Em	F♯°	G	Am	Bm	C	D

Can you spot the modal interchange in Fig. 100?

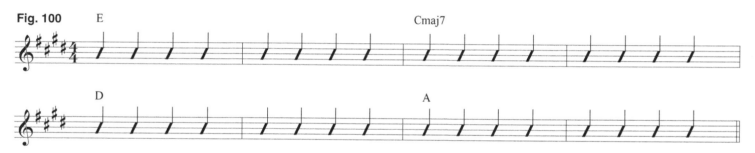

If we compare these chords with Fig. 97 we see that E and A are from E major (they are the I and the IV) while the Cmaj7 and D chords are from E minor (they are the VI and VII in E minor).

Now I'll give you a solo example over this progression.

59 **Fig. 101 – Modal Interchange in E**

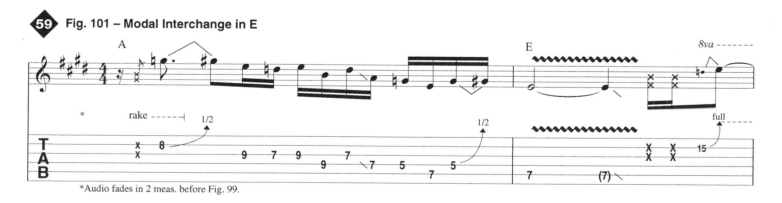

*Audio fades in 2 meas. before Fig. 99.

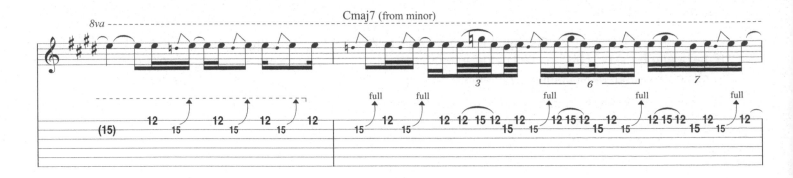

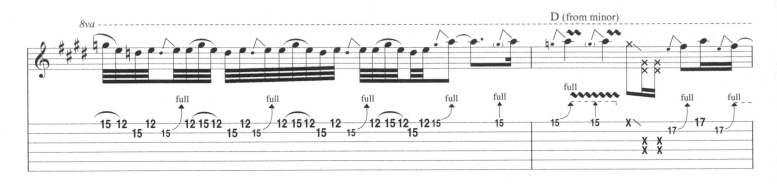

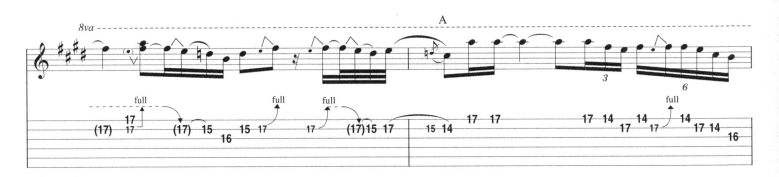

Here's a challenging one in A:

60 **Fig. 102 – Modal Interchange in A**

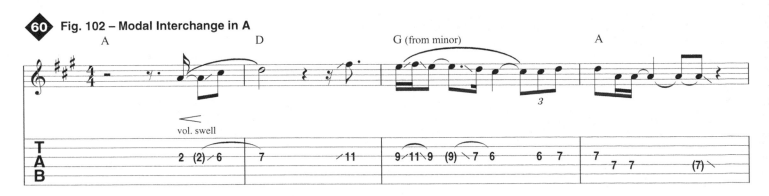

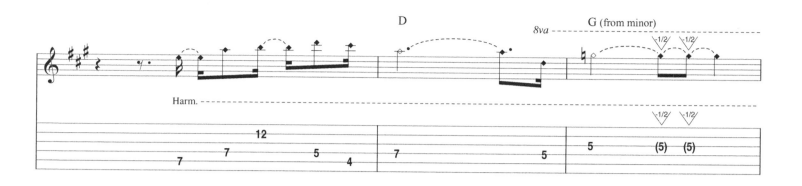

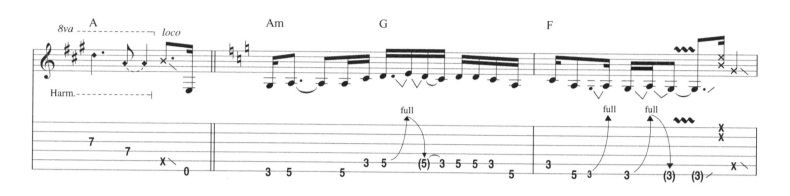

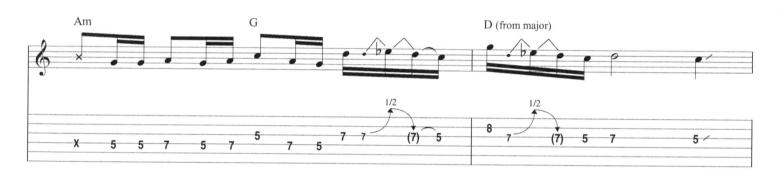

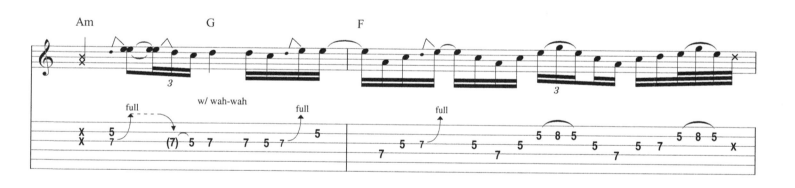

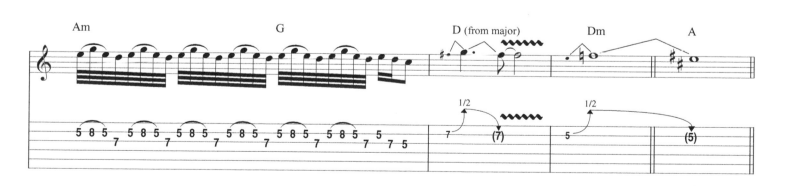

Now you try…

61 **Fig. 103 – Modal Interchange Jam in A**

Here's another example. The F♯7 chord is from the key of B major (F♯ Mixolydian or E Lydian).

62 **Fig. 104**

*Audio fades in 1 meas. before fig. 102.

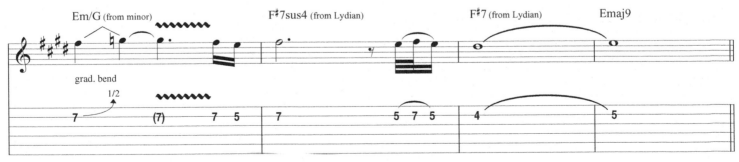

And now it's your turn:

 Fig. 105 – Jam Track for More Modal Interchange in E

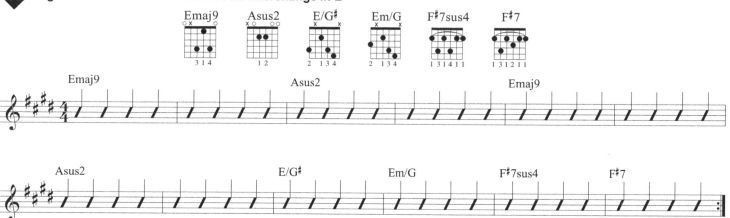

SECONDARY DOMINANTS

The word "dominant" has been used throughout the book as a shorter name for the dominant seventh chord (1–3–5–♭7). But the word originally meant "the chord in the fifth position." It so happens that, in a major key, the V chord is a 1–3–5–♭7 chord. That's how the name *dominant seventh* came to represent a 1–3–5–♭7.

A *secondary dominant* is a V chord of a chord other than I. Below is a song using a secondary dominant chord.

Fig. 106

Looking at the key of C, one of these chords clearly doesn't belong.

Fig. 107

I	II	III	IV	V	VI	VII
C	Dm	Em	F	G(7)	Am	B°

The D7 chord is not in the key. Where does it come from? Here's the answer: *it's the V chord of the G chord;* D7 is V in the key of G. Grab your guitar and strum through the chords. Notice how the D7 pulls your ear towards the G chord. This is a secondary dominant and we call this the five-of-five (V/V). The other dominant seventh chord (G7) is the normal dominant chord (also called the *primary dominant).*

Guess what scale you would use to solo over that D7?

Answer: G major

Do you know a better name for the G major scale at that moment?

Answer: D Mixolydian (since it's a D chord, you should call your scale D also—it helps you remember that D is important.)

Fig. 108

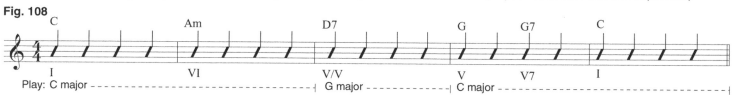

Let's try another in the key of C.

Fig. 109

Which chord doesn't belong?

Answer: E7

E7 is a V of what chord?

Answer: Am (V/VI)

What scale do you play for an E7 chord in A minor?

Answer: A harmonic minor.[5]

Fig. 110

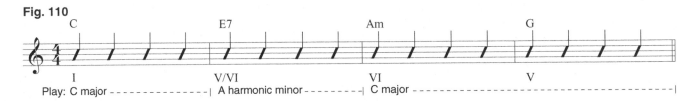

Here are five short progressions showing you all of the secondary dominants in the key of C. Secondary dominants can happen quickly because they are usually passing chords. You might only have time for a couple of notes, so you might as well make them the important ones. Which notes are the important notes? The notes in the secondary dominant chord.

Fig. 111 – Secondary dominants in C

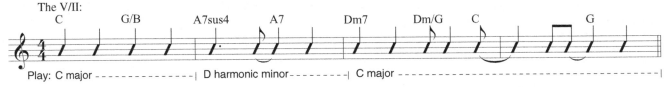

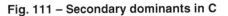

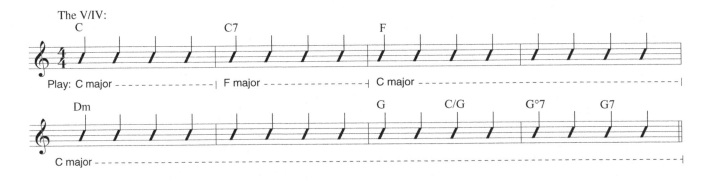

---

[5] E7 is the V of the VI chord. In our key (C major), the VI chord is Am. So E7 is the V chord in the key of A minor. You learned earlier in this chapter that, in minor keys, you have to play harmonic minor for dominant V chords. So, when your secondary dominant is a V of a minor (V/II, V/III, or V/VI) you'll need to use a harmonic minor scale for your solo.

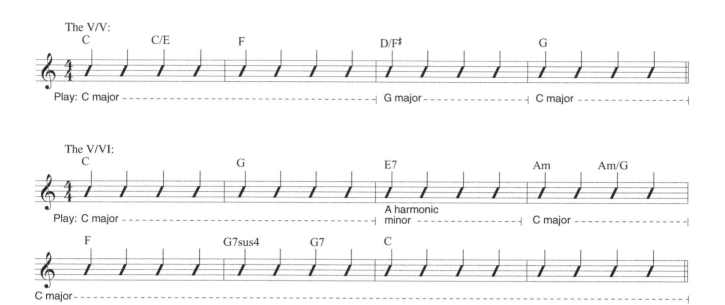

Now I'll show you some soloing possibilities over the last five figures, and give you a chance to jam over the rhythm tracks on the second time through each figure.

64 **Fig. 112 – V/II Solo and Jam**

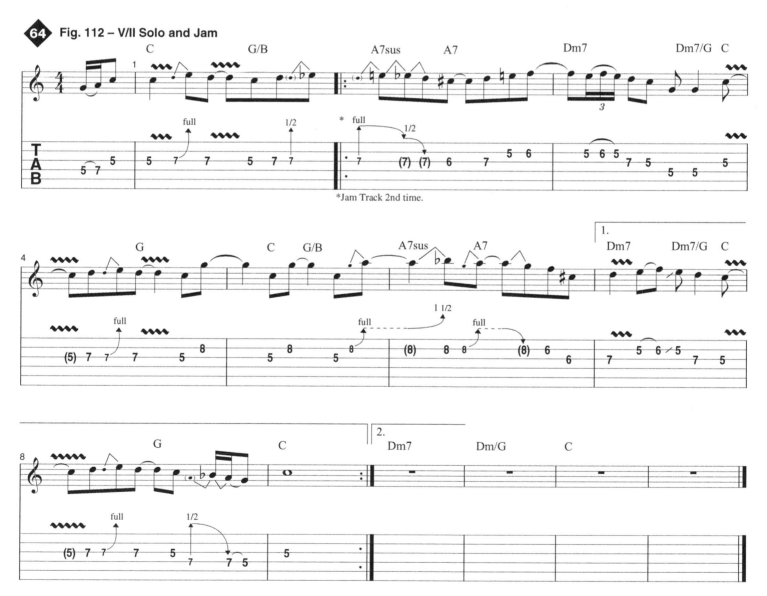

*Jam Track 2nd time.

Notice the use of D harmonic minor in measures 2 and 6 of Fig. 112. The E♭s in measures 1 and 2 are chromatic passing notes—don't dwell on them. I was just playing by ear.

65 Fig. 113 – V/III Solo and Jam

*Jam Track 2nd time.

Check out the D♯ in measure 1 of Fig. 113. That's the harmonic minor scale! Notice that I didn't play a D♯ in measure 5. If you hit it every time, it can be predictable. The F♯ and B♭ in measure 8 are chromatic passing notes again.

*Jam Track 2nd time.

I played the C Mixolydian scale verbatim in measure 2 of Fig. 114. Measures 4 and 5 are a statement; measures 6 and 7 are a reply to that statement.[6] Also check out the B♭ in measure 10—C Mixolydian right where it's supposed to be!

67▸ Fig. 115 – V/V Solo and Jam

*Jam Track 2nd time.

Watch the F♯s in measure 3 of Fig. 115. That's the D Mixolydian scale (D–E–**F♯**–G–A–B–C–D).

68▸ Fig. 116 – V/VI Solo and Jam

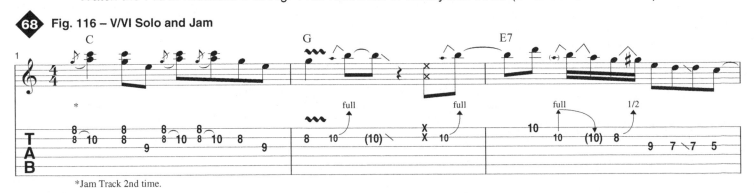

*Jam Track 2nd time.

[6] For more on "statements and replies" or call-and-response, see *Rock Lead Guitar Techniques*.

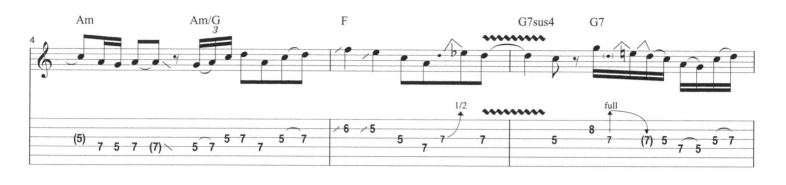

*Hold previous bend with 4th finger and add pinky on the 11th fret.

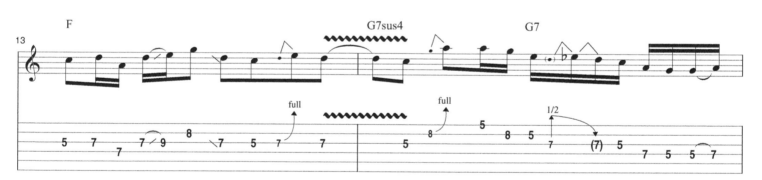

I used the bluesy harmonic minor scale in measure 3 of Fig. 116. In measure 11, I used the regular A harmonic minor scale (the important note—G♯).

In case you're wondering, there is no V/VII.

MINOR KEY APPLICATION

You can use secondary dominants in minor keys, too. Below is an example, but before you start, take a look at the scale changes—pretty quick, huh? Just be ready to hit the important notes. For example, the important note for the G7 chord is F♮. Why? Here's why:

Our key—E minor

E–F#–G–A–B–C–D–E

G Mixolydian

G–A–B–C–D–E–F–G

The *only* difference between the two scales is that G Mixolydian has F♮. That's why it' so important.

69 Fig. 117 – Secondary Dominance in a Minor Key

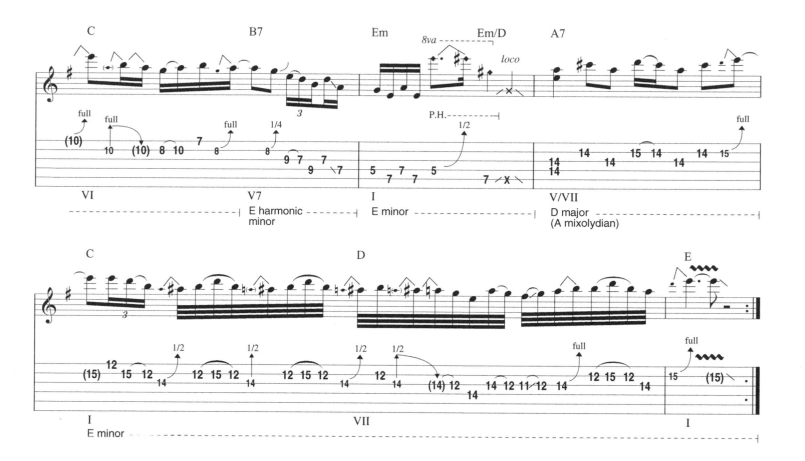

CHAPTER 5
BLUES-BASED MUSIC

So far we've discussed about everything you'll run into in the rock world: modal interchange, secondary dominants, modulations…all the "thinkin' stuff." This final chapter is going to take a look at the easiest stuff to hear but the hardest stuff to analyze: blues-based music.

Let's get familiar with the basic form of the blues—the 12-bar blues.

Fig. 118 – 12-Bar Blues in E

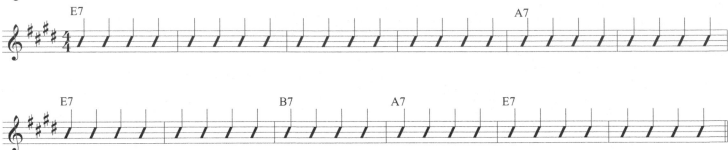

The I, IV, and V are all dominant seventh chords! This is a theory nightmare! How come this all sounds like one key? E sounds like home the whole time—so these aren't modulations. They're not secondary dominants (because A7 is V of D and there isn't a D chord in E major). It seems none of the theory we've discussed will answer this.

Well, it's time to take the thinking caps off and just do some playing. If you listen to the blues dating all the way back to the very first recordings, you'll notice that most of the vocal melodies and soloing is derived from these notes: 1–♭3–4–♭5–5–♭7. It's called the *blues scale*.

Fig. 119 – Blues Scale Patterns

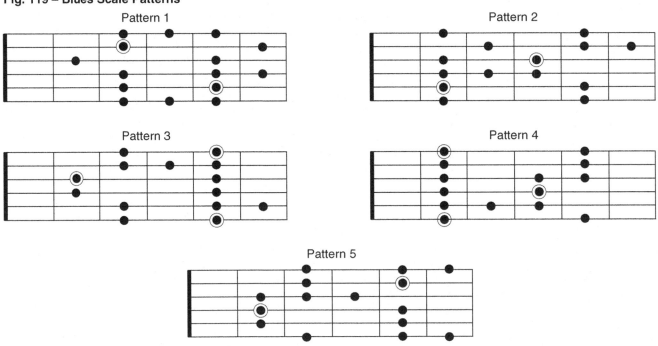

You'll notice that these scales are just minor pentatonic scales with the addition of a ♭5. The ♭5 is called the *blue note* because it has a sad quality. It's a good idea to become familiar with all five patterns, but I'd be lying to say that every good blues player uses all of them. Most use patterns 2 and 4.

Exercise: Your ear is your most important tool when playing the blues. Play along with the track. I'll fill the first twelve measures with a very basic blues solo. I want you to emulate that solo on the rest of the chorus. We're not going for flash here. Your goal is to mean what you play—it doesn't matter how hard it is. Don't over-think the blues— just let it happen.

Fig. 120 – 12-Bar Blues in E (Solo and Jam)

*Jam Track on 2nd & 3rd times.

I hope you noticed something on the solo of Fig. 120. The notes of the blues scale were not strictly followed. There was one bend in particular that you should look at. It was the G (fifteenth fret, first string) bending up to G♯. I did this on the first note of measure 3. Most players do this without even knowing it, because it sounds good. Why does it sound good?

Think about the E7 chord: E–G♯–B–D.

When you play G over this chord, you naturally want to bend it up to G♯.[7] That is simply paying attention to the "major-ness" of the E7 chord. Continue practicing until you master this all-important bend.

---

[7] We touched on this already—back in modes and the bluesy harmonic minor.

GOING FURTHER

So far, we've dealt with the real blues (I7, IV7, and V7). Let's take what we've learned there and apply it to some different situations.

Here's a straight-ahead rock progression in E that uses some modal interchange (the G and D chords are from E minor). Let's think like a blues player and mush all of the chords into one basic key. We'll think in E blues. Keep in mind some of the things you learned in the previous examples: try to bend your G up to G# on the E chord.

71 Fig. 121 – Rock 'n' Roll in E (Solo and Jam)

PLAYING BLUES IN MAJOR KEYS

So you're Joe Blues-Man—got your shades and Telecaster—but the singer wants to sing a pretty little ballad in D major and you don't want to blow your cool…what do you do?

You see, the major scale is just a little too cute for most blues players, so they'll play most of the song in major pentatonic and throw in some of the minor pentatonic (with some creative bending) to get that "sassy" sound. This is not called breaking the rules—it's called *destroying* the rules! Playing a minor scale on a major song?!? Pay close attention to the transcribed solo—it sounds great, but it ain't easy.

72 Fig. 122 – People Get Set

*Jam Track 2nd time.

from minor pentatonic

*Slide and bend simultaneously.

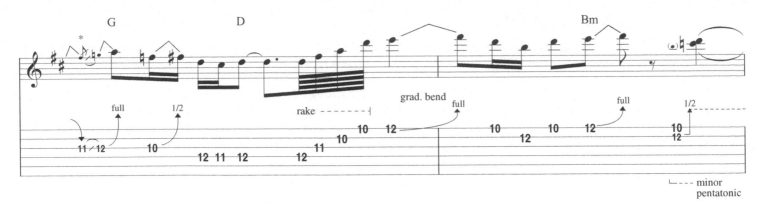

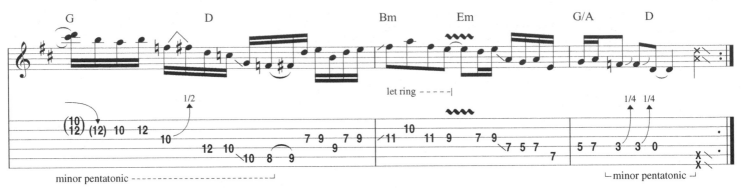

Here's a recap for you. If you can master this one, we'll call you when we need a sub at MI!

The first eight measures are basically a really long A7 chord. You've learned that you can play a Mixolydian scale over that. Also, you could think like a blues player and play an A blues scale (with that minor third to major third bend). Try major pentatonic if you like.[8] Next is a modulation to C major. I chose to make a "statement and answer" in my solo. I wonder what you're going to do. In measure 13, there's another modulation—this time to D major. Try out some of the modulation techniques you've learned. In measure 15, it modulates to a G7 chord. There's a lot of action coming from the band, so I try to keep it sparse. Have fun with this one and we'll see you when you get to MI!

73 **Fig. 123 – Final Solo/Jam**

---

[8] If you've forgotten about major pentatonic scales, go back and take a look at *Rock Lead Basics*.

GUITAR NOTATION LEGEND

Guitar Music can be notated three different ways: on a *musical staff*, in *tablature*, and in *rhythm slashes*.

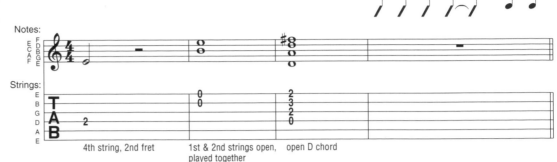

RHYTHM SLASHES are written above the staff. Strum chords in the rhythm indicated. Use the chord diagrams found at the top of the first page of the transcription for the appropriate chord voicings. Round noteheads indicate single notes.

THE MUSICAL STAFF shows pitches and rhythms and is divided by bar lines into measures. Pitches are named after the first seven letters of the alphabet.

TABLATURE graphically represents the guitar fingerboard. Each horizontal line represents a string, and each number represents a fret.

4th string, 2nd fret   1st & 2nd strings open, played together   open D chord

HALF-STEP BEND: Strike the note and bend up 1/2 step.

WHOLE-STEP BEND: Strike the note and bend up one step.

GRACE NOTE BEND: Strike the note and bend up as indicated. The first note does not take up any time.

SLIGHT (MICROTONE) BEND: Strike the note and bend up 1/4 step.

BEND AND RELEASE: Strike the note and bend up as indicated, then release back to the original note. Only the first note is struck.

PRE-BEND: Bend the note as indicated, then strike it.

VIBRATO: The string is vibrated by rapidly bending and releasing the note with the fretting hand.

WIDE VIBRATO: The pitch is varied to a greater degree by vibrating with the fretting hand.

HAMMER-ON: Strike the first (lower) note with one finger, then sound the higher note (on the same string) with another finger by fretting it without picking.

PULL-OFF: Place both fingers on the notes to be sounded. Strike the first note and without picking, pull the finger off to sound the second (lower) note.

LEGATO SLIDE: Strike the first note and then slide the same fret-hand finger up or down to the second note. The second note is not struck.

SHIFT SLIDE: Same as legato slide, except the second note is struck.

TRILL: Very rapidly alternate between the notes indicated by continuously hammering on and pulling off.

TAPPING: Hammer ("tap") the fret indicated with the pick-hand index or middle finger and pull off to the note fretted by the fret hand.

NATURAL HARMONIC: Strike the note while the fret-hand lightly touches the string directly over the fret indicated.

PINCH HARMONIC: The note is fretted normally and a harmonic is produced by adding the edge of the thumb or the tip of the index finger of the pick hand to the normal pick attack.

PICK SCRAPE: The edge of the pick is rubbed down (or up) the string, producing a scratchy sound.

MUFFLED STRINGS: A percussive sound is produced by laying the fret hand across the string(s) without depressing, and striking them with the pick hand.

PALM MUTING: The note is partially muted by the pick hand lightly touching the string(s) just before the bridge.

RAKE: Drag the pick across the strings indicated with a single motion.

TREMOLO PICKING: The note is picked as rapidly and continuously as possible.

VIBRATO BAR DIVE AND RETURN: The pitch of the note or chord is dropped a specified number of steps (in rhythm) then returned to the original pitch.

VIBRATO BAR SCOOP: Depress the bar just before striking the note, then quickly release the bar.

VIBRATO BAR DIP: Strike the note and then immediately drop a specified number of steps, then release back to the original pitch.